# WAR IN EUROPE

Adolf Hitler's fanatical thirst for empire,
the courageous resistance it provoked,
and the titanic battles that ravaged a continent are now brought to breathtaking
life in this remarkable new series by noted
historian Edwin P. Hoyt. Here is the un-
forgettable story of World War Two in the
European theater—a detailed, dramatic
and astonishing military chronicle of victory and defeat in the brutal struggle between the forces of freedom and tyranny.

## VOLUME THREE

## THE BATTLE OF BRITAIN

VOLUME THREE

# WAR IN EUROPE
## THE BATTLE OF BRITAIN

# EDWIN P. HOYT

AVON BOOKS NEW YORK

I am indebted to a number of people for assistance in the preparation of this book, particularly Bud Hough, who shared with me some of his knowledge of the Battle of Britain, and archivists at the Imperial War Museum in London and at the Public Records Office in Kew. Librarians at Mathews County (Va.) Library were also extremely cooperative in finding and getting books from interlibrary loan services.

WAR IN EUROPE VOLUME THREE: THE BATTLE OF BRITAIN is an original publication of Avon Books. This work has never before appeared in book form.

AVON BOOKS
A division of
The Hearst Corporation
1350 Avenue of the Americas
New York, New York 10019

Copyright © 1992 by Edwin P. Hoyt
Published by arrangement with the author
Library of Congress Catalog Card Number: 91-93018
ISBN: 0-380-76482-2

First Avon Books Printing: March 1992

Printed in the U.S.A.

RA 10 9 8 7 6 5 4 3 2 1

# CONTENTS

# PROLOGUE

August 12, 1940. The German Luftwaffe prepared for *Adlertag*—Eagle Day—the day on which the pulverization of the Royal Air Force would begin with the destruction of the British radar installations on the coast that could give early warning to the RAF and allow the fighter groups to send squadrons up to intercept the German bombers.

But how were the Luftwaffe bombers to find their targets?

There was the secret, kept for many months by the Germans and now to be used in the all-out offensive that was to precede Operation Sea Lion, the invasion of England by the German army, which was being prepared for early September. The secret was a radio beam which the Luftwaffe bombers could use to home on any given target and which would make their bombing effective in any kind of weather. It was called the Knickebein, and the Germans were confident that the British would never discover its secret, at least not until it was too late.

On June 27 the British intercepted a secret coded message, and by use of the Enigma code machine, which was a rebuilt German model, they were able to decode the message that it was proposed to set up "Knickebein and Wotan."

So the day was coming closer and the danger was increasing.

On July 21 General Ernst Milch, the German chief of the air staff, met with Reichsmarschal Hermann Goering.

"We can achieve air supremacy only by destroying the

RAF and its supporting aero-engine industry.''

As to the tactics, the factories had to be the focal point, along with the radar and air installations. And as the battle began, the Knickebein was the secret . . .

# CHAPTER 1

# Reality and Myth—
# the Truth About
# Air Power

In the manner of Jules Verne, the enthusiasts for air power began in the 1920s to build a myth, not entirely inappropriate, that air power would decide the future of the world. Billy Mitchell, American army general and one of the prime proponents of air power, was so elated by his enthusiasm, and so bedeviled by his opponents, that he went too far (at least for his time) and suggested that bombers could sink battleships, a bit of lese majesty that ultimately brought about his downfall although he was quite right in his basic premise. But in the 1920s it was not definitely proved and certainly not generally believed by the military men. However, the air power men, as opposed to land army generals and naval admirals, overstated their case. One major effect was to frighten half the world that a new war would bring a sort of world holocaust by bombing.

During World War I, the Germans had used both airships and bombers to attack England, but with little real damage because of the limited carrying capacity of the aircraft of the period. After World War I, one of the principal noisemakers about air power was Italy's Mussolini, who promoted the view that air power would decide the fate of nations in the years to come, and backed up his words with a demand on the Italian Chamber of Deputies in the spring of 1927 for the most powerful air force in the world. The deputies believed, and Italy began to build a powerful air force.

That view was seconded in England and the British Empire by Jan Christian Smuts, the old Boer leader who had a great deal of influence on Winston Churchill. Another who adopted the militant view of air power was Adolf Hitler, spurred on by his association with Hermann Goering, one of the air heroes of World War I. But Hitler's view was that air power was a powerful adjunct to land power—that the airplane could be used to subdue the enemy in a blitzkrieg—lightning attack.

Mussolini tested his theories first in Abyssinia, where his aircraft made satisfactory attacks on the mud cities of Haile Selassie. He and Hitler again tested their theories in Spain, when Guernica was destroyed, and Madrid and Barcelona were maimed by bombers. In the 1930s the British accepted this view that bombing could decide the outcome of a war and began to build their air power accordingly. But they built heavy and medium bombers, while the Germans, especially, never built a heavy bomber. Even the leaders of the British opposition Labour party believed that another world war would mean the end of the world.

Also in the 1930s, on the other side of the world, the Japanese were attacking the Chinese cities with bombers after the China war began in 1937, and the photos and newsreel footage of these attacks were convincing evidence that if war is hell, air war is the inferno. After the war began on September 1, 1939, the British began to move people, mostly women and children, out of London. Soon a million and a half had been moved out. But the bombs did not come immediately, either on the British or on the Germans, because each side was so much in fear of retaliation by the other that both the Luftwaffe and the RAF held back. The first British flights over Germany were confined to reconnaissance missions. All during the winter of 1939 and 1940, people in Britain and Germany waited, but the bombs did not fall. It was as if there were some unwritten conspiracy between the war leaders to try to avoid the holocaust they expected when and if the bombing did begin. There were a few tentative attacks, but they seemed to have been limited to overenthusiasm by airmen, as on March 16, 1940, when a bomber dropped a bomb toward shipping in Scapa Flow and killed a cottager, and another instance on May 9, when apparently two villages near Canterbury were attacked without casualties. By June 1940, Britain was prepared for bombing, with a compulsory blackout all across the country, but no bombers.

Then in the summer of 1940 the approach to bombing changed. Air Marshal Goering, in preparation for the forthcoming invasion of Britain that Hitler planned, with the fall of France, set out to harass British shipping and production facilities. He assured Hitler that the full force of the Luftwaffe alone could bring the British to the point of surrender. And what of the weapons of the two sides?

In 1934, just after the Japanese had walked out of the League of Nations over the Mukden incident, just after Hitler had come to power with his promise of revenging Germany for Versailles, just as Mussolini was preparing to seek his empire in Africa, Britain began to expand her air force. A new scheme set up a target of seventy-five home defense squadrons to be achieved in five years. But in 1935 Hitler let it be known that the Luftwaffe was already stronger than the British Royal Air Force and was going to build much more strength. The British response was to add squadrons to the plan until they would have 112 squadrons by March 1937.

So, too, was the British bomber force increased, and new airfields were built in East Anglia, and fighter squadrons began to be moved toward the coast, all the better to intercept possible enemy aircraft. In another shift, the potential enemy was identified as definitely Germany, whereas before 1935, France had been perceived as the possible enemy in the British war plan.

The Royal Air Force was reorganized, too, into fighter command, bomber command, training command, and coastal command. This structure was in effect at the outbreak of the war.

And what of the enemy?

When Air Marshal Sir Hugh Caswall Tremenheere Dowding set up the fighter command headquarters at Bentley

Priory, in the suburbs of London, the Germans were admitting that the Luftwaffe was one year and four months old. Even before the official admission of the existence of the Luftwaffe in 1935, the Germans had 584 combat aircraft and a monthly production of about 180 aircraft. That was to be increased to the eve of war to 3,600 fighting planes, plus 550 transports and a monthly output of 700 aircraft. And all this was done in secret. After 1935 it was all still secret, and no budgets for aviation spending were ever issued.

The training of pilots had begun a long time ago, during the days when theoretically the German air force did not exist and when theoretically there could be no air training except for transport pilots. All of these things were controlled under the Versailles Treaty by the international commission set up to police German air activity.

The secret was to train glider pilots, which was legal. By the middle of the 1920s there were hundreds of glider pilots. And what did they know? They knew their aerodynamics, and knew how to handle an aircraft in the air. To be sure, they had not yet been exposed to power-driven heavier-than-air craft, but this was essentially not very difficult. A pilot who could fly a glider could very quickly become adept with a power-driven aircraft. All the essentials were there, and perhaps because of the difficulties, more than with the British, the German fighter pilots certainly proved to be very proficient in World War II. Among these pilots, the most skillful, who took tests to prove their skills, were selected by Lufthansa, the German airline, for further training programs. Lufthansa maintained a number of flying schools, and in reality was a sort of air academy, with definitely military traditions on the ground in matters of discipline and behavior, which were quite unusual for a civilian airline.

By 1932 the Lufthansa training program included aerobatics and maneuvering that no sane airline would ever employ. The Germans were training fighter pilots.

In 1933, after Hitler took power, some of these pilots were sent to Italy to train under Italian command. In 1934 the organization of the Luftwaffe began with the selection of the first class of pilots to receive infantry training and be given a commission in the German army. By 1935 Lufthansa had established what was really a highly specialized school for fighter pilots. That year the Luftwaffe became official, Hermann Goering designed a new striking blue uniform for the new air force, and Germany was displaying a force that had been off and running for five years.

The Germans by this time had another advantage: they were becoming involved in combat. In the outbreak of hostilities in 1936, when General Franco challenged the republic, the Germans flew ten thousand troops from Morocco to Spain. From then on, the Germans were in the air and fighting. The Legion Kondor was established to help Franco win his revolution. German pilots were sent to Spain in relays, to get into combat, gain experience, and come home to instruct the next group. In Spain they were flying Heinkel 51 fighters and Messerschmitt 109s. So already in the late 1930s the Germans had tested superior aircraft, and tested superior pilots, ready for war.

While the Germans were developing the Heinkel and Messerschmitt fighters and other special fighting planes, the British were concentrating on the development of two basic fighters, the Hurricane and the Spitfire. The British had developed a superior aircraft fighter engine, the PV 1200 Merlin, which was used in both the Spitfire and the Hurricane and later in the American P-51 fighter. The British were also working on a new fuel, a one-hundred-octane aircraft fuel, which they would bring into play in 1940. The Germans did not learn this secret until late in the summer of 1940 when they analyzed the fuel from a crashed British fighter. But it was one thing to find out what the enemy was doing and another to do it, so the Germans continued to be behind, in terms of aircraft performance due to fuel. This disparity was partly made up by the essential superiority of the ME-109 in performance before the fuel change. When Hitler marched into the Rhineland, the Spitfire was already going into production. In 1939 two thousand Spitfires were on hand, and the Hurricane, which was unveiled in 1938, was also in full production. For the Germans by 1939, the ME-109E was in production, and this, too, was a very fast, very maneuverable, and very stable aircraft. The ME-109E was usually armed with two wing cannons of twenty millimeters each, plus two

7.9-millimeter machine guns, roughly equivalent to .30-caliber. Messerschmitt was also producing the twin-engined ME-110 fighter, which had a range of 565 miles and a speed of 350 miles per hour at twenty-three thousand feet. The ME-110 carried a crew of two.

Fortunately for Britain, the Germans failed to produce a heavy bomber, so great was their emphasis on the air force as a sort of air artillery, to further the advance of the army. Therefore Germany went into World War II with only twin-engined medium bombers as their strongest weapon, and thus were no match for the bombardment capacity of the British or American air forces. This was to tell the tale in the end, but it was not to affect the Battle of Britain except to limit the payload and effectiveness of the German bombing campaign.

The most common bomber that appeared during the Battle of Britain was the Heinkel HE-111, a design that dated from the earliest days of the German air expansion. It was a single-wing, all-metal aircraft with twin engines, which carried a crew of four and could deliver more than two tons of bombs. Its speed was about 250 miles per hour, and it carried three 7.9-millimeter machine guns. The first machines were not armored, but as they faced the powerful British fighters and were shot down, the Germans began to add armor for protection of gas tanks and the crew members.

Another German bomber that would appear in the skies above Britain was the Dornier DO-17, a high-winged, twin-engined monoplane which had a speed of 250 miles per hour and a very small bomb load, just over two thousand pounds.

The third twin-engined German bomber was the Junker JU-88, which was also the best. This was a low-wing twin-engined plane, which had a range of six hundred miles and a load of two tons. The JU-88 could make 286 miles per hour and was armed with three machine guns. It was fast and durable and could dive away from enemy fighters.

Another famous German aircraft that would participate in the battle of Britain was the JU-87, the Stuka dive-bomber, which had terrorized the world during the first days of the war. The Stuka had been extremely effective in Poland and against horse cavalry and infantry on foot, with its characteristic screaming dive. But the battle of Britain found a more formidable foe in the British fighter, and the Stuka would prove ineffectual except in the attack on merchant ships because it was too slow for the air war of 1940 at two hundred miles per hour and not easily maneuverable. It was designed to pinpoint and hit a fixed target, and could not easily swerve once committed. So the Stuka's life in the battle of Britain was to be short and limited.

So as the clouds of war formed over Europe in the politicking and appeasement of 1938, the two air forces prepared for the battle. In Britain there was considerable fear of the horrors of an air war, voiced most vociferously by Stanley Baldwin, who warned that the bombers would always get through in the coming battles and that the only defense in air war was a good offense. He forecast a war of horror, waged against women and children—and as it turns out, he was almost exactly right.

But although the British people did not know it (nor did the Germans), by 1935 the British had found a way of detecting the approach of hostile aircraft which would work in storm or fog or dark of night. Radar was being born. It would be the most significant development in the Battle of Britain, and in the end would foil the German effort to destroy the fighter capability of the Royal Air Force.

By 1936 radar and the Spitfire and Hurricane fighters together gave Britain an edge on the defensive side, but the production was still extremely limited. In 1937 the decision was made at the cabinet level to build a chain of twenty radar stations, an expensive decision, because it was estimated to cost a million pounds at a time when money for defense was hard to come by. By January 1937 it was obvious in England that the German air effort was being stepped up, and the Air Ministry proposed the strengthening if the RAF wanted to add five hundred planes to the force, but the government of Neville Chamberlain was demanding "business as usual" and did not want to spend the money on defense. Winston Churchill was demanding a buildup of defense in Parliament, but the Chamberlain government was resisting stoutly. Because of these debates, by 1938 Britain's military was committed to a purely defensive posture by the beginning of World War II. (This accounts for the British refusal, and particularly the RAF refusal, to commit British air forces fully to the joint battle with the French against the German breakout in the spring in Belgium and northeast France, and the subsequent defeat and fall of France.)

By 1938, however, the foot draggers in the Chamberlain government were finally convinced that the war was inevitable and that Britain must do more than shore up its old defenses. It must plan not just to fight and defend Britain, but ultimately to win a war.

The world has blamed Neville Chamberlain for "appeasement" of Germany in the negotiations at Munich that led to the partition of Czechoslovakia, but the answer is not as simple as it seems.

When the Germans pushed their way into Austria in the spring of 1938, Chamberlain called on his chiefs of staff for advice. What was Britain to do if Hitler threatened Czechoslovakia, as he was already talking about doing?

The chiefs of staff told Chamberlain that there was no way to stop Hitler swiftly at this point. "No pressure that we and our possible allies can bring to bear either by sea, on land, or in the air, could prevent Germany from overrunning Bohemia." The chiefs of staff also told Chamberlain bluntly that Britain was not prepared for the sort of war that would defeat Hitler. The army was too small, the RAF was too weak, the navy could not carry the war alone.

Thus Chamberlain was warned that he had no recourse but to use his powers of negotiation to forestall Hitler's advance. Hitler, of course, sensed Britain's weakness, although he did not know the details, and thus Chamberlain's negotiations came to nothing. But while Chamberlain was negotiating buying time, the British war machine was moving into gear. The real complaint should have been, why did it take them so long? And that had to be answered by citing the preoccupation of Britain, France, and America with the domestic problems of the great depression of the 1930s, which transcended all else, preventing the Western allies from stopping the Japanese advance in the Far East as well. What Winston Churchill referred to as "the powers of darkness" had the advantage; they controlled their economies and could manipulate their civilian populations, while the Western democracies were dependent on public support, which had to be rallied through reason and exposure to the wrongdoing of the Germans, Italians, and Japanese. It was a time-consuming process, and the problem was that by 1938, there was no time left.

In the spring of 1939 the British program was still almost totally defense-oriented. At first, when the military men contemplated sending an expeditionary force to fight on the continent if war came, they allocated four fighter squadrons to the task. Everyone knew it was not nearly enough. In May 1939 the number was raised to ten squadrons.

By September 1939 some five thousand pilots were in training. The big problem was in defense against enemy attack, with only two-thirds of the needed number of searchlights available, and only 695 heavy antiaircraft guns, although 2,300 were needed. Night antiaircraft guns were even scarcer, only 253 available although 1,900 were needed.

But in one area the British were doing very well: civil defense. In 1938 there simply was no system, but by 1939 a million and a half men and women were enrolled as air raid wardens, and in the fire and ambulance services, Hundreds of street shelters had been prepared.

In August 1939, without fanfare, the British began to mobilize for war, as Hitler ranted and raved against Poland. Gas masks were distributed to the public. Women and children in the most threatened urban areas were being moved to the country. The blackout was imposed everywhere. In the hospitals, beds were emptied of chronic and short-term patients to make room for 150,000 casualties expected from German air raids as soon as war began. Radar had been extended to cover most of the country that was threatened, and new airfields had been built to house fighters to meet the German bomber threat. In September 1938 the number of fighter squadrons had been twenty-nine, of which only five had Hurricanes. All the rest had outmoded biplanes that could not stand up to the modern Luftwaffe attackers. But in 1939 four squadrons were assigned to the expeditionary force destined for France, and there were still thirty-five squadrons left for the defense of the home area; seventeen were Hurricane squadrons and twelve were Spitfire squadrons.

# CHAPTER 2

# *The Respite of Phony War—and Its End*

On September 3, 1939, Britain declared war on Germany. Hitler had ignored the repeated warnings that unless he desisted in his attack on Poland, the British and French would go to war. And so war came.

Hardly had the prime minister completed his broadcast to the nation announcing the war when the British air raid warning system swung into action. An unidentified aircraft had crossed the Kentish coast and brought the air defense to condition red; fighters took off from southern airfields to investigate, and in London, government workers and others moved down into the air raid shelters.

But it was all a false alarm. The Germans were not attacking; the aircraft was a friendly civilian plane from France, heading for Croydon.

Several times that day civilian aircraft whose flight plans had not been announced to the authorities frightened up the red warning system. In the next few days there was a lot of confusion in the air defense system, and on September 6, Hurricane and Spitfire fighters scrambled from different fields, got into a fierce battle, and two Hurricanes were shot down by Spitfires. The RAF came to call it ruefully the Battle of Barking Creek, and the affair was soon known around

England, and was the subject of a good deal of cynical laughter.

But every day the pilots grew more adept at aircraft recognition, and more skillful. They were lucky to have the time, due to the quiet of the war fronts. Hitler still hoped that once Poland had been defeated in the "blitzkrieg" in the east, Britain and France would be persuaded to abandon the war and let him go his own way, swallowing Europe at his own deliberate speed. The British and French governments had no such intention, but they were not ready to strike a blow at Germany. The British expeditionary force had first to be assembled, and then sent to France and put in place. The French were content to view the world defensively from behind the Maginot Line.

And the Germans had to reorganize their panzer division, and move many thousands of troops from the eastern front to the west. So from September 1939, when the defeat of Poland was accomplished really in little more than a week, the war wound down, and during the autumn and winter of 1939 and 1940, the only war that was real was the sea war, with Admiral Karl Doenitz's U-boats raiding the waters around Britain and laying mines as well as torpedoing vessels. Indeed, in this period the mining was more effective than the torpedoes, although two aircraft carriers were attacked, one was sunk, and the battleship *Royal Oak* was also sunk by a German U-boat.

In the air, the war proceeded at a leisurely pace. On October 16, nine JU-88 bombers attacked the British fleet elements at Rosyth, and British fighters shot down two of them, the first German planes to be destroyed over Britain since 1918.

The occasional German air raid yielded some valuable information to the British. One bit was taken from an He-111 bomber, which was equipped with a system using a radio beam to direct its flight and bombing. This was immensely useful to the British.

For the most part, though, the RAF involvement with the enemy concerned the chase and sometimes fights with German planes going after British shipping.

It was a slow war. Most of the German attacks took place along the east coast of Britain; very little action was observed over the English Channel, because this was a long haul from German fields. The first fight over the Channel occurred in late March 1940, when the merchant ship *Barn Hill* was set afire by bombs from Luftwaffe bombers.

By the end of March 1940 the Germans had sent some four hundred flights over Great Britain and had lost about forty aircraft. The British had lost no fighters. Still the RAF was troubled, because of the shortage of fighter aircraft that Air Chief Marshal Dowding saw. More squadrons were being added, and more old squadrons were being reequipped with Spitfires and Hurricanes. Also there were changes coming to the RAF defense, bulletproof windshields for the aircraft, and armor plate behind the pilot's seat to prevent him from being shot in the back.

Also, the radar system was made stronger and the stations more numerous. British planes were fitted with an electronic "Identification: Friend-or-Foe" device that helped prevent incidents of British planes shooting down their fellows.

During this period the RAF resisted as much as it could the demands of the army and their French allies for air support of the British expeditionary force. Four squadrons of fighter planes had originally been allocated to this task, the release of them much lamented by Air Chief Marshal Dowding. Two more squadrons were allocated.

In September 1939 Dowding figured that he needed fifty-seven squadrons to provide proper defense of Britain. At that time he had thirty-nine squadrons. Then the Germans began beefing up the Luftwaffe, and the need rose to sixty squadrons to counter a German bomber force of more than two thousand planes.

There was very little air action over the French front in the fall and winter of 1939-1940. The first German plane was shot down on October 30, 1939. For eight months of quiet, then, there was little air activity. The first serious activity came when the Germans and the British simultaneously decided that something had to be done about Norway. April and May of 1940, then, the RAF had to provide pilots and planes to cover the British land and sea operations in Norway, and the RAF lost three squadrons of planes in the process.

Then in the second week of May 1940, the phony war

ceased to be phony. The Germans began moving on May 10. The British sent four more fighter squadrons to reinforce the six squadrons then in France. From virtually no air activity, the situation changed within hours, and the men of Squadron No. 3, sent over from England on short notice, found themselves immediately in combat, not once during the day, but three times. The pilots of No. 607 Squadron fought nine times that day, and some of the pilots made as many as seven missions in that one day.

The British ground forces moved swiftly into Belgium to counter the German offensive. Prime Minister Chamberlain resigned and was replaced by Winston Churchill. During the first seven days of the intensive fighting, fifty Hurricanes were lost, and although more German planes were destroyed, still Air Chief Marshal Dowding was concerned about the ratios. His overweening worry was the protection of Britain from a massive German bombing attack, and he felt that his resources were strained much too greatly to assure his success.

From the first day of the offensive, the fighting was furious. The British planes that first day escorted the French Seventh Army, flying forty-four sorties along the Scheldt River estuary, and fought German bombers upon the beaches near the Hague.

On the second day the pressures on Air Marshal Dowding grew stronger. The Belgians, the Dutch, the French, were all calling for more British air fighter support, and that would have to come from Dowding's reserves, held for British protection.

The matter went to the War Cabinet, which decided to send thirty-two more Hurricanes, as individuals, not squadrons. But that did not help much. By May 14 the cry reached its highest level when that evening French Prime Minister Paul Reynaud called for ten more fighter squadrons to stem the German breakthrough of the Allied lines south of Sedan, in the attempt to cut the Allied lines in France in two.

To the French appeals were added those of the British army expeditionary force. Air Marshal Dowding tried to resist all these importunities, and when the War Cabinet next met in a few hours, he made his case that to continue to send fighter planes to France would be to weaken the home defenses to the point that they might not succeed at the hour of need.

But in those desperate days of May, opinions changed almost from hour to hour. In a few hours Churchill decided that six squadrons should be sent to shore up the French. The cabinet balked and would only send four squadrons, but they were sent.

Prime Minister Churchill had gotten it into his head that Britain only required twenty-five squadrons of fighters to oppose the Germans at home, a figure dredged from a long-ago time, 1938 perhaps. But in 1940 the figure was much greater because of the constant building of the Luftwaffe, and Air Chief Marshal Dowding knew it. So he continued to resist the demands, and the demands continued to come as France was in desperate straits.

On May 16 Churchill attended a meeting of the Allied war council in Paris. From Paris he called for another six squadrons of fighters to be sent to France. Following that cry, three more squadrons were detailed to fly from England during the morning, operate for several hours in France, and then fly back to England in the evening.

But by that time, May 17, the whole Allied position was collapsing and General Guderian's panzers were cutting across France and heading for the English Channel. The British sensed that the battle was lost, and on May 19 and May 20 the British fighter planes were all withdrawn from France and sent back to England, a move the French considered to be abandonment of them in their most desperate hour. But the decision had been made in London: No more fighters would be sent to France, no matter how loud the cry, no matter how desperate the need.

On May 21 the German panzers reached the mouth of the Somme at Abbeville, and cut the Allied forces in the South from those in the North. Within hours the British began to move toward Dunkirk, and now British fighter command was called on to give more support by fighters. The fighters responded: On May 23, Group II, which provided the fighters for this defense, flew 250 sorties and lost ten pilots. The next day Squadron 54 sent its planes against seventy German bombers near Dunkirk and then attacked twelve ME-109s near Calais. Another ten pilots failed to return that day.

On the night of May 26 came Operation Dynamo, the evacuation of Dunkirk. That day Marshal Goering announced that his Luftwaffe single-handedly would cut the British defense forces to ribbons, and the Luftwaffe came in force from bases in Holland and France as well as from Germany. To oppose this the British had only sixteen squadrons made available. On May 27 the British flew 287 sorties and claimed thirty-seven German planes shot down, while losing fourteen British fighters. But on the beaches, the troops saw the Luftwaffe and they did not see much of the RAF.

For the next few days the British flew three-hundred sorties a day, but the Luftwaffe still scored many successes, sinking steamers, sinking and damaging destroyers to the extent that the Royal Navy became vitally concerned about the future of the destroyer force.

On the night of June 2 the evacuation of Dunkirk was complete, but many thousands of French had to be taken off according to agreement with the British. Luckily the next two days offered terrible flying weather over the English Channel, so the evacuation continued with very little air activity on June 3 and June 4. By the end of June 4, 338,000 troops had been taken off, most of them without any of their equipment, but they were off and could fight again. By the end of that day, although Dowding held back from total commitment, every Hurricane and Spitfire fighter squadron in England except three had taken some part in the effort. The fighting was good for the training of the pilots, but also the loss of pilots and planes was serious.

When the battle ended on June 4, in the House of Commons Prime Minister Churchill gave fulsome thanks to the RAF for winning a victory over the Luftwaffe, making the successful evacuation possible. But it was exaggeration. To be sure the RAF had inflicted some losses on the Luftwaffe, shooting down two hundred aircraft and three hundred air crew members, but his statement that the RAF was far superior to the Luftwaffe was not quite factual, or if the RAF was then superior, it had not yet proved itself.

From June 5 onward, the British air defenses' effort in France lessened, in spite of desperate calls from the French. Fighter planes were still in France, but no more were being sent. On June 13 Churchill promised the French that ten squadrons of fighters would operate over France from British bases. For a few days this was tried, but soon the battle was so obviously lost that the fighters concentrated on the protection of the last British forces and the west coast ports, as the British waited to get out of France.

On June 17 the French requested an armistice with the Germans, and it was all over then for the British in France. The fliers left as swiftly as they could and headed back to England.

It was time, then, to total the losses and make some assessments. The Luftwaffe had lost 1,300 aircraft in this battle just concluded, and that represented about a third of its total strength employed. The British had lost more than 950 aircraft, or about half the strength of the RAF at the beginning of the German offensive. Almost as severe, great quantities of spare parts and equipment for the Royal Air Force had been abandoned in France and would have to be reconstituted, at the expense of building new. One squadron of Blenheims had lost twenty-six air crews and had only six of its original crews left.

The Germans were smarting, and needed time to rebuild their forces. But so did Britain. The question was: which side would do so better and quicker?

# CHAPTER 3

# *The German Juggernaut*

With the fall of France in June 1940, Hitler then had to decide how he was going to deal with Great Britain. The escape of the vast majority of the British expeditionary force to go home, reequip, and fight again was a great blow to the German hopes of a quick victory. Hitler felt that the British were defeated, but would not quit. He tried to convince them that this was the case, without any success at all. Almost in his first day of office that spring of 1940, Prime Minister Winston Churchill had warned the Germans that Britain would never give up, and the basic reason that the Royal Air Force was not fully committed to the joint operations against Germany was that the British military command never trusted the ability of the French, or their willingness to fight and win, and so the great bulk of British air strength was held back, as was naval strength, for home defense.

Actually, in May the British chiefs of staff had seen what was coming more clearly than the political leaders. At least in May they came to the proper conclusion, that Hitler would attempt to finish off Britain in the next few months. They believed then, or they did not care, that the Germans would turn against Britain before France. But the outcome was the same, and because the chiefs of staff were overwhelmingly concerned with defense and not offense, they made preparations that perhaps did not suit the joint war effort of France and Britain, but did begin the buildup of home defenses. Consequently, by the second week of May, Britain was gearing up for defense against a major German attack.

In the middle of May the British government created a new Ministry of Aircraft Production, to cut through red tape and speed up the building of military aircraft. Lord Beaverbrook was chosen to be the minister, and within a few hours he had set the wheels in motion to increase the production of bombers and fighter planes. The then plan of production for fighter planes for May was about 260. The actual output was more than 300 planes. The goal for June was slightly under 300 planes. The actual was nearly 450 planes. That figure was maintained for the next two months. So as the battle of Britain loomed in the summer of 1940, Britain was far better prepared for it than the Germans had ever dreamed they would be. Hitler and Goering in June 1940 thought they faced a nation that was at least half-beaten. They were in for a big surprise.

By the end of May, the British chiefs of staff were expecting the fall of France, and they prepared for a fight in which they would have to stand alone. They saw in the air force and navy their first line of defense against a possible invasion by the Germans. And so did the Germans see in the air force and navy the first line of defense. By the time France fell, Hitler was already planning the invasion of Britain, although hoping that he could convince the stubborn English that their cause was lost and they had best surrender. Admiral Erich Raeder, the German naval chief, was very much opposed to such an invasion as impractical. He did not have the landing craft or the capital ships to stand up against the Royal Navy. But Goering assured Hitler that this was all unimportant, he would so batter Britain's air defenses that they would disappear. Then the problem of the British navy could be solved by the joint efforts of the Luftwaffe and the German navy, and the invasion could go on as planned. In his more fervid moments, Goering predicted that the Germans could simply walk ashore and take over, so completely would British defenses be destroyed.

Facing the bleak prospect of fighting alone, the British war planners predicted that Britain could ultimately win such a war, with several important provisions. One was that they secure the economic support of the United States in increasing amounts. Another was that they withstand the immediate battering that was to come in the German effort to bring a quick end to the European conflict. If those conditions could be met, they felt, their imposition of an economic blockade of Germany, plus the buildup of resistance movements in the occupied countries, and a sustained bombing attack of Germany, would ultimately bring victory over Hitler.

By July the Germans were making obvious moves toward building up a sea force to invade Britain. The Channel ports were tightened and closed to observation as small craft were assembled. Meanwhile in Berlin the army, navy, and Luftwaffe planners continued their discussions about the invasion, where, when, and how.

The how was the biggest difficulty. The army wanted to invade on a broad front that spread all around southern England. But the navy said the ships could not be found, and the landings could not be protected against the ravages of the British Royal Navy. So the army plans were scaled down, but still the navy protested.

The key, it was soon seen, was the ability of the Luftwaffe to control the skies above Britain and thus pave the way for the sea and land offensive. The German problem was that after the battle of France, the German air force needed some time to regroup, reorganize, and secure new aircraft and fresh pilots.

By the first of June, Hitler had ordered heavier air attacks on Britain, in order to prevent the British air force from attacking the German production facilities in the Ruhr. By July 2 the army had convinced Hitler that an invasion of Britain was possible, and Goering's braggadocio about his Luftwaffe was generally believed.

On July 16 Hitler issued the orders for Operation Sea Lion, the invasion of Britain, although he accompanied it with ''an appeal to reason'' and peace, which meant peace on Hitler's terms. This appeal was rejected by the British once again, specifically by Lord Halifax, the foreign secretary, in a broadcast speech.

In July the Luftwaffe began concentrating its attacks on

British shipping, as the first step in weakening Britain for the invasion. It was called the *Kanalkampf* by the Luftwaffe, and by July 20 most of the strength of the Luftwaffe was employed. The three air fleets that comprised the operational arm of the Luftwaffe in the west were employed. *Luftflotte* 2 was in the charge of Field Marshal Albert Kesselring, based in France north of the Seine, Belgium, Holland, and northern Germany.

*Luftflotte* 3 was commanded by Field Marshal Hugo von Sperrle, and it was located in western France. *Luftflotte* 5 was under General Hans-Juergen Stumpff, located in Denmark and Norway.

The three *Luftflotte* could put up against England nearly thirteen hundred bombers, three hundred dive-bombers, and more than one thousand fighter planes. They also had observation planes and other specialized aircraft.

On the British side that summer, the strength of bomber command was not very important, for the bombers would not figure in the struggle for the defense of Britain against the German onslaught that was expected. What was important was the British fighter strength, and since May this had been recognized and every sinew was being strained to strengthen that fighter force.

Earlier Air Marshal Dowding had called for fifty-two fighter squadrons. By July he had fifty-two squadrons, with three more in the process of working up. He had eight hundred fighters to oppose the German bombers and fighters, but one hundred of them were old-fashioned Blenheims, not suitable for the job ahead. They were valuable these days as night fighters.

The British fighters were organized into four groups. Group II with its headquarters at Uxbridge guarded the southeast part of England to Suffolk County. It was commanded by Air Marshal Keith Rodney Park, a New Zealander. This group had twenty-two squadrons with 350 aircraft; thirteen squadrons were equipped with Hurricane fighters, six with Spitfires, and three with Blenheims. Most of these squadrons were placed on fields in a ring around London.

On the west was located 10 Group, with headquarters in Wiltshire, commanded by Air Vice Marshal Sir Quintin

Brand, comprising in July about sixty aircraft in seven squadrons.

North of these groups was 12 Group in Nottinghamshire, which covered the British midlands. It was made of thirteen squadrons: six Hurricanes, five Spitfires, one squadron of Blenheims, and one of outclassed Defiant fighters. The commander was Air Vice Marshal Trafford Leigh-Mallory.

The final group was 13 Group, which had its headquarters at Newcastle on Tyne, which covered the north, Edinburgh, and the British naval base at Scapa Flow. It had twenty-two squadrons of Hurricane fighters, six of Spitfires, one of Blenheims, and one of Defiants. Air Vice Marshal Richard Saul was the commander. This was the fighter defense circle, and at its center was the operations room at Bentley Priory, which gathered information about enemy activity and sent it to the air groups, which then got through to the squadrons on the airfields.

Bentley Priory's operations room was built around a large table, covered by a map of the area. Around it stood the operators, with headsets and wands, moving the plots of enemy aircraft across the board. Above the scene sat the officers who controlled the air force. And tied in with this system were the civil defense and the antiaircraft guns.

By the beginning of the second week of July, these forces were arrayed and the Battle of Britain was ready to begin.

# CHAPTER 4

# *The Battle of the Convoys*

As July began, it was apparent in England that something big was about to happen. In the first few days of the month it became evident that the Germans had begun to concentrate their aircraft on the newly captured and repaired French airfields that were so much closer to England than to Germany. On July 3 planes from Belgian airfields struck British airfields. On July 4 Stuka dive-bombers, as part of the operation against coastal shipping, attacked a coastal convoy and all but decimated it. But the day selected by the RAF as the beginning of the Battle of Britain was July 10, 1940.

July 10 dawned wet and murky. Early in the day, Blenheim squadrons were prepared for attacks on German airfields at Amiens and Saint Omer, but the weather was so filthy that the pilots did not really expect to fly that day, nor did the British fighter pilots in their fields scattered across England. But in spite of the driving rain, at seven-thirty that morning the action began with a telephone call at Coltishall Airfield in Norfolk, where Squadron 66 was located. A three-plane section of Spitfires was ordered to take to the air and intercept an unidentified aircraft reported off the coast.

The three Spitfires took off and climbed up through a heavy cloud layer to break into the summer sunshine above. They were directed to the area where the "bandit" was spotted, and at eight-fifteen pilot officer Charles Cooke saw what he identified as a Dornier 17 bomber. This was a reconnaissance flight; it had little chance against three Spitfires, although the pilot and crew did their best, and a burst from the DO-17's guns caused one fighter to turn away. But the other two shot the plane down and it fell into the sea near Yarmouth, killing the four crew members.

Pilot officer Cooke's plane had taken that burst of fire from the DO-17, and the windshield had been half blown away, but he managed to bring the plane down safely, and the other two pilots were in fine fettle.

By nine o'clock that morning the weather had begun to clear, and the gray skies were replaced by a patchy network of blue. Off the English coast another Dornier 127 spotted a convoy heading southwest of Dover. The crew radioed the position, course, and speed back to the airfield.

The Dornier was picked up by the British radar stations, and so was a squadron of ME-109s that was flying top cover for the observation plane. When the word reached the base, Manston fighter command scrambled three Spitfires to attack. The three British planes found the Dornier and attacked and were in turn "bounced" by the ME-109s up above. The Spitfires got through to the Dornier and shot it up so badly that it lost altitude as it fled across the Channel toward Boulogne, where it crash-landed, with a dead pilot and several wounded crew members.

But the word about the British coastal convoy had reached the German airfields. Field Marshal Kesselring sent a whole squadron of ME-109s to draw off British fighters and give the German bombers a good chance at this convoy. This squadron took off from France just before ten-thirty that morning and swept across the Channel at low level to the cliffs of Dover, when they were picked up by Spitfires which took off from the airfield at Biggin Hill and intercepted the German planes. But they failed to do anything spectacular, although the British leader was wounded so badly that he had to make a forced landing.

The Germans continued on, to draw RAF activity away from the convoy in the Channel. At one-thirty that afternoon the real attack on the convoy began, and soon the Dover radar station showed much German air activity behind Cap Gris Nez. What appeared soon enough was a force of twenty-four Dornier bombers, in V formation, escorted by twenty ME-110s, and about twenty ME-109s flying top cover at twelve thousand feet. Two squadrons of Hurricanes went to the attack, Squadron 111 and Squadron 32. Also in came the Spitfires of Squadron 74. As the Germans came over Dover, two of the Spitfires damaged two of the Dorniers right above the town, and the antiaircraft guns began spotting the sky with big black bursts and lines of tracer bullets. Nine Hurricanes attacked in a line, and broke up the formation of Dornier bombers. One Hurricane, piloted by Thomas Higgs, collided with one of the bombers, and both planes fell to the ground, taking to death all but two of the crew of the Dornier, but also killing Higgs. Another Dornier was chewed to pieces by several Hurricanes.

The German bombers tried to get at the convoy, which was not far from Dover, and the British fighters tried to keep them away. The ME-110 twin-engined fighters formed into tight circles so that their rear gunners could fire on the attacking British fighters, but soon the attacks were pressed so fiercely that the German planes headed back across the Channel, in small groups of ME-110s, groups of ME-109s, and Dorniers. Three more Hurricanes were damaged in the fight, one of them by an overeager Spitfire pilot, but the convoy escaped with the sinking of one small ship.

That same day, bombers from *Luftflotte* 3 headed for Swansea and Falmouth in western England. They were sixty-three JU-88s, and to confuse the radar, they approached the Cornish coast from the west. The ploy worked and the British Spitfire fighters stationed at Penmbrey Airfield were slow to take off because of it. The German bombers bombed their targets without interference and then headed back across the English Channel to France.

There were eight British coastal convoys at sea this day, July 10, and German reconnaissance planes were looking for them to bring German bombers in. Several convoys went undetected, hidden by cloud cover. But the Germans made themselves felt in this first big raid of the campaign to destroy

British shipping, and the following day the British newspapers were full of stories about the exploits of British fighter pilots and the damage done to port facilities and to one convoy by the enemy. A dozen German planes were shot down by fighters and antiaircraft fire, and another ten planes were damaged. The British lost only the single fighter pilot, Higgs.

Next day, July 11, the Luftwaffe came again, and this time the major burden was carried by the Stuka dive-bombers against convoys in the West. The first Stuka raid was attacked by Spitfires from Squadron 609, but when the Spitfires came roaring down on the slow German dive-bombers, they in turn were hit by three flights of MEs which were flying cover up above. Two British pilots were shot down and killed. Later in the day came another raid, these Stukas supported by twin-engined ME-110 fighters. But the German fighters were too high and had not reckoned with the slow speed of the Stukas and the greater speed of the Hurricane Squadron 601, which attacked them over Portland. Two Stukas were destroyed and two ME-110s, while the other ME-110s were helpless to stop the fighting—too far from the scene. The Hurricanes flashed after the other Stukas, and the pilots jettisoned their five-hundred-pound bombs and fled homeward across the Channel.

The next day, July 12, the Germans were back again to attack a convoy off the east coast of England. In this attack the German bombers made good use of formation tightness and gunnery accuracy to shoot down two of the attacking Hurricanes of Group 12, and damaged several other fighters without losing any German aircraft.

For the next week flying was kept to a minimum by heavy weather over the Channel, but on July 19 came an incident that proved once and for all the unsuitability of the Defiant fighters. These planes had been brought into service in 1935, two-seater fighters with a revolving turret, which mounted four machine guns. The plane had no forward-firing fixed machine guns, so the pilot could not fire, but had to depend entirely on the skill and resources of the gunner. This weakness was amplified by a blind spot beneath the tail, which the Germans soon found, and learned to come up underneath to attack in the blind spot, where they were not bothered by return fire.

Squadron 141, which was equipped with Defiant fighters, was moved to Hawkinge in July, and on July 19 nine of them were sent aloft to protect convoys. It was a clear day, and that meant the ships and aircraft protecting them could expect trouble from the Germans.

Shortly after noon the nine Defiants were in the air, patrolling south of Folkestone. Suddenly, without any warning, they were hit by a flight of ME-109s.

The gunners began swinging their turrets, but then another flight of ME-109s joined the fight, and the Defiants began to fall one by one as the fighters found their weak spot. Fortunately for three of the nine crews, the Hurricanes of Squadron 111 arrived and three planes made it back to Hawkinge, but one of the three Defiants was so badly damaged that it would never fly again, and one of the gunners was killed.

By July 19 it was clear that the Luftwaffe was bent on the destruction of local shipping around Britain. That day Hitler arose in the *Reichstag* and made another "peace offer," although he had already ordered the preparations for the invasion of Britain. In these nine days the air activity had been as great as the weather permitted. On July 10 the Luftwaffe made that first big attack, losing thirteen planes to the RAF's six. In the raid of July 13, the Germans had sacrificed seven planes to the RAF's single loss. On July 14 off Dover, the RAF had lost four planes and the Germans only two, but the next day the Luftwaffe had lost three planes to the RAF's one. On July 16 the ratio had been three Luftwaffe planes shot down to the RAF's loss of two. On July 17, when the Luftwaffe attacked shipping off Dundee and Beachy Head, they lost two more planes and the RAF lost one.

On July 18 it rained all day, not heavily, but the rain came down. The Luftwaffe was out again, although some of the airfields on the French side of the Channel were so waterlogged that many planes could not take off. The same situation prevailed on the British side, hampering the air defenses. That day the Luftwaffe lost four planes and the RAF lost three.

Then came the day that the RAF learned that the Defiants could not hold their own.

The raids continued, beginning the twentieth, the day after Hitler's new "peace offer." There was a new fillip now, the use of the ME-110 as a fighter bomber, not just as a fighter. The Luftwaffe was learning that the ME-110 did not hold its own well against the fast and maneuverable British Hurricanes and Spitfires. The Germans raided the Liverpool area that night seeking shipping, and they lost nine aircraft while the RAF lost three.

The twenty-first day of July dawned clear and bright and brought heavy German attacks on shipping in the Channel. The British fighters were up, and they shot down nine German planes, losing six in the process.

On July 22 the air activity was somewhat restricted although the weather was clear with a few showers, an indication perhaps of the waiting of the Germans for the British reaction to the new "peace feeler." But when it was resoundingly rejected, as noted, on July 23 the Germans were back with attacks on east coast shipping. July 24 brought heavier attacks, with a loss of eight German planes in attacks on convoys in the Channel and the destruction of three RAF planes.

July 25 brought another new wrinkle, a combined attack on a convoy by the Luftwaffe and German E-boats. This attack was carried out by several squadrons of JU-87 Stukas and their losses were heavy, eighteen planes shot down to seven RAF fighters. But the real loss to Britain was in the convoy, where eleven of twenty-one ships were sunk by the combined attack. This result was so serious that the Channel convoys were suspended during the daylight hours to prevent recurrence of such disaster.

The Germans were getting the hang of it, learning to attack ships more successfully from the air, and on July 27 two destroyers were sunk by German bombers.

The Germans had been meeting to plan for more effective attacks on British shipping. The commanders of the three *Luftflotte* were assembled by Goering and instructed to increase the activity and the successes. Goering had been talking to Admiral Raeder and had agreed to intensify the laying of mines in British ports, with submarines from Admiral Doenitz's command also increasing their activity in this regard. The idea was to close the ports and the passage of convoys up and down the British coast. Goering pointed out that these attacks were valuable to Germany in damaging British shipping, and also valuable to the Luftwaffe in helping train crews in closer cooperation between bombers and fighter planes.

Field Marshal Kesselring continued the pressure despite his heavy losses, particularly on July 25 when wave after wave of Stukas hit that large convoy off Dover in conjunction with the E-boats. Also the big coastal guns on Cap Gris Nez were now brought in to join the fight. This fight of July 25 was in some ways the most memorable yet of the air war. The Stukas were so numerous, as well as the escorting ME-109s, with the odds four to one against the British.

It was apparent that the Germans were stepping up the level of their activity seriously. On July 28 the Germans hit hard on shipping off Dover, so hard that the Royal Navy withdrew its destroyers from Dover to Portsmouth at the end of that day. The Germans lost heavily, eighteen planes shot down to the RAF's three. The British could see that the loss ratio of aircraft for the RAF over British soil was low, and the other great advantage was that RAF pilots who could crashland on British soil were ready to fight again almost immediately, while Germans shot down became prisoners of war.

On the bright morning of July 29 the Luftwaffe sent a heavy concentration of Stuka dive-bombers, some fifty in all, protected by eighty ME-109s, to attack the harbor at Dover and two convoys just outside the harbor. As the battle developed, almost two hundred aircraft were diving and swirling above the town, and the antiaircraft guns were blasting away, firing at anything that moved, so that the effect was of a giant maelstrom.

In the first phase of the battle, four Stukas were shot down and one Spitfire was destroyed, and many planes on both sides were damaged.

The second phase of the battle began with a German attack on one of the convoys by a large force of JU-88s, guarded by ME-109s and ME-110s. This force was the *Erprobungs-*

*gruppe* 210, a highly trained unit, which would appear from time to time in the next weeks. The Germans attacked a sixty-ship convoy off the Thames Estuary. They sank a few small ships, but the worst loss was a destroyer. The Germans paid that day with eight aircraft destroyed.

Next day, July 30, Goering warned his Luftwaffe that the real battle of Britain was about to begin and that they must be prepared to carry on the fight ceaselessly with twelve hours notice. That day again the Luftwaffe raided shipping off the east coast of England, did not sink any ships, and lost five aircraft. That day at Hitler's retreat near Munich, Admiral Raeder said firmly that he would not be prepared to launch the invasion of England before September 15. Hitler was annoyed but agreed that September 15 would be the day, but it was understood that the air offensive against England would begin about August 5, and on its outcome would depend the final decision for the invasion.

When the RAF counted the results of this first phase of the battle against shipping, it came out that the British had lost sixty-nine fighter planes between July 10 and July 31, and had shot down 155 aircraft. The Germans had sunk eighteen small coastal cargo vessels, larger cargo ships, and four destroyers.

The British did not know that the battle was entering its second phase, but on August 1 Hitler ordered it: "In order to establish the conditions for the final conquest of England, the Luftwaffe will overpower the English air force with all the forces at its command in the shortest possible time."

First the attacks would be directed against the fighter bases and the aircraft in the air and on the ground, the aircraft industry, the supply lines, and manufacturers of aircraft equipment. Only after the Luftwaffe achieved air superiority would they return to the attacks on ports and the shipping. Hitler reserved for himself one decision, whether to convert the attack against military targets to an attack on civilian populations and a campaign of terror.

Following the conference with Hitler, Air Marshal Goering issued his own directive. For the first five days of the assault the Luftwaffe would concentrate on targets within 150 kilometers in the area south of London. For three days after that, the Luftwaffe would aim at targets closer to London, and for five days the attack would center on the area around London, close in, within fifty kilometers of the city.

The assault was to be called *Adlerangriff*—Eagle Assault. It would open with *Adlertag*, Eagle Day, the first good day near August 5. After the Eagle Assault, Goering boasted, the army and the navy would simply walk in, and Operation Sea Lion would be nothing but an exercise.

But as far as the RAF was concerned, August 1 came, and with it a continuation of the shipping strikes of the Luftwaffe. These attacks would continue for the next two weeks.

So on August 1 the Luftwaffe hit shipping off the south and east coasts of England, losing nine planes and shooting down one RAF fighter. Next day, which was drizzly offshore, they again hit shipping off the southeast coast. Result: four Luftwaffe planes lost.

On August 3 the Luftwaffe lost four planes in the Liverpool area, without hurt to the RAF.

For the next three days there was little activity; the Luftwaffe lost seven planes and the RAF two. On the third day, August 6, Goering gave orders for *Adlertag*: it would be on August 10.

On August 7 the Luftwaffe hit a convoy off the east coast, losing two aircraft. But on the following day, August 8, the Germans made heavy attacks on a westbound convoy off Dover, which involved the heaviest air fighting of the campaign thus far, with about 150 aircraft involved. The Stukas attacked at night and proved very vulnerable. The Germans lost thirty-one aircraft to the loss of twenty RAF fighters.

The next day, August 9, was so rainy and stormy that *Adlertag* was postponed from August 10 and the Luftwaffe confined itself to attacks on barrage balloons around Dover, with a loss of five aircraft to the RAF four.

August 10 proved to be as dirty a day as the meteorologists had predicted, and there was virtually no air activity anywhere, with no casualties on either side.

August 11 was a fine day, and the Luftwaffe was out in force, over Dover and Portland in convoys off the east coast. That night other planes hit the Liverpool area and the Bristol

Channel in heavy attacks, but thirty-eight German aircraft were shot down, while thirty-two RAF planes were lost.

In these first preparatory days for the cross-Channel attack, the Germans had attacked shipping steadily, laying mines as well, and sinking thirty thousand tons of shipping, but this was a small loss considering that five million tons of ships passed around the coasts of Britain in this period. Luftwaffe losses were 286 planes for the period of this first phase as compared to 150 RAF planes.

On August 12, in preparation for the great day, the Luftwaffe plastered RAF airfields in the southeast, hitting especially the fields at Manston, Lympne, Hawkinge, and doing serious damage to the British radar stations at Dover, Rye, Dunkirk, and Ventnor. To accomplish this, the Germans sacrificed thirty-one aircraft, and the RAF defenders lost twenty-two planes.

The attack at Dover was accompanied by shelling from the long-range coastal guns in France. At the end of the day, Field Marshal Kesselring had very satisfying reports from his commanders. General Wolfgang Martini, head of the signal section of the Luftwaffe, reported that the attacks had been 75 percent successful. Four sections, each of four fighter bombers, ME-110s, came from east of Calais at just about eight-thirty in the morning. The attack force broke into its four sections over southeast England. One hit Dunkirk, northwest of Dover. When they reached Dunkirk they bombed, and the raid was on the radar installation targets.

The second target was the Pevensey radar installation; the third was near Rye, and then Dover itself.

At Pevensey the results were spectacular: the concrete building collapsed like paper towers, the lines were knocked out, and the main supply cable was destroyed.

At Rye every hut was also destroyed by the German bombs.

At Dover the damage did not seem so serious.

Later in the day Marshal Kesselring tested the efficacy of his raid by sending several attacks on convoys in the Thames Estuary using Stukas, which had proved to be very vulnerable to British fighter attacks.

The Stuka attack was unhampered by British fighter opposition because, for the first time in weeks, the radar system was not operating efficiently. The Foreness station near the Thames Estuary was not hurt, but that station could not do the job all alone, and the British fighter groups were not given adequate information to find the enemy. The fighters arrived late, but they did arrive at the convoy between Deal and Ramsgate, and a melee ensued. A mixed force of Hurricanes came up, and lost four planes to the German fighters lurking up above.

Also that night the Germans launched a heavy attack on the south coast, to test the radar—100 JU-88s and 120 ME-110s, with another 25 ME-109s hitting the British naval bases at Portsmouth, and Portland, industries at Portsmouth, and the Spitfire Supermarine engine works at Woolston.

So the attacks on the radar stations, the Luftwaffe commanders agreed, had been successful. As one commander put it, "The RAF's eyes have been put out." But that night Kesselring ordered further tests of the British defenses by sending three raids of some twenty Dornier bombers each to coastal towns, all of them with fighter escort. All three raids were picked up by the British before they even left the French coast, and it was obvious that the British defenses were not destroyed. Radar stations had been hard hit and had lost many personnel. But by hard work, before the night was over, radar stations at Hawkinge and at Manston were back on the air, and so were the others except for Ventnor, which had been hardest hit of all.

And so that night, at its bases in France, Germany, the low countries, and Norway, the Luftwaffe waited for the word from its commander, Marshal Goering, and it came.

"TO ALL UNITS OF AIR FLEETS TWO, THREE, AND FIVE, OPERATION EAGLE. WITHIN A SHORT PERIOD YOU WILL WIPE THE BRITISH AIR FORCES FROM THE SKY."

Next day would be the day of decision.

# CHAPTER 5

# *The Secret Radio Beam*

In the winter of 1940 a young British scientist named R. V. Jones was studying new German weapons to see how they might work and how they could be counteracted. One day he received a message from RAF air intelligence telling about a new X-Apparatus that had been discussed privately by two German prisoners of war who did not know their conversation was bugged. What was said indicated the apparatus was used in a bomber and that it involved radio pulses.

Dr. Jones heard nothing more of this until one day in March a German Heinkel 111 bomber was shot down. It had the call sign 1H + AC, which showed that it was from the bomber group *Kampf Geschwader* 26. Inside was a fragmentary entry in a log.

> Navigational Aid: Radio Beacons working on Beacon Plan A. Additional from 0600 hours Beacon Duehnen. Light Beacon after dark. Radio Beacon Knickebein from 0600 hours on 315°.

Dr. Jones concluded that Knickebein was some sort of beamed beacon which that day had been set to transmit in a northwesterly direction. With this information those two prisoners were again interrogated, and intelligence confirmed that the X-Apparatus was indeed a beacon sent by shortwave, which would not be more than a kilometer wide over London.

But that was all that could be learned. The war proceeded. The Germans began their attack on the low countries and France in the spring, and by June, France was finished and the British troops were fleeing from Dunkirk.

Then on June 12 an RAF officer showed Dr. Jones a scrap of paper.

"Does this mean anything to you?"

KNICKEBEIN, KLEVE, IST AUF PUNKT 53 GRAD 24 MINUTEN NORD UND EIN GRAD WEST EINGERICHTET.

CLEVES KNICKEBEIN IS ESTABLISHED AT POSITION 53 degrees 24 minutes NORTH AND 1° WEST.

That geographical position was a point in England on the Great North Road, a mile south of Retford. So Dr. Jones knew the Germans had a Knickebein radio beam transmitter set up at Cleves, on the point of Germany nearest to England, and the existence of the beam over England had been confirmed, probably by a flight of a bomber.

This was part of a message decoded by the Enigma machine, a message sent by the chief signal officer of *Fliegerkorps* IV.

But again, that was all.

Dr. Jones made it a point to find out what sort of bombers *Fliegerkorps* IV used. They were Heinkel 111s of *Kampf Geschwadern* 4 and 27. He telephoned air intelligence and arranged for prisoners from Heinkel 111s to be interrogated, and this was done. The prisoners denied knowing anything about any beams. But when the interrogation was ended, the prisoners were again alone, and again their conversation was recorded:

"No matter how hard the English look, they will never find it."

"*Ja.*"

Dr. Jones knew he was on the right track. He secured a copy of the technical report on the Heinkel 111 shot down on a raid on the Firth of Forth, and studied it. The only item he saw that might apply was a special receiver carried by the aircraft for the purpose of blind landing. This sort of receiver was commonly in use all over Europe.

But Dr. Jones telephoned to the expert who had evaluated this equipment.

"Is there anything unusual about the blind landing receiver?"

"No." Then there was a pause. "But now that you mention it, it is much more sensitive than they would ever need for blind landing."

So Dr. Jones knew that the Knickebein receiver was masked as Blind Landings receiver Type 1, and he also knew the frequencies on which it could be tuned.

A day or so later, a new prisoner confirmed the fact that the Knickebein was a bombing device, which involved two intersecting radio beams. The prisoner also drew a sketch of Knickebein transmitting tower, and Jones recognized it from photographs as one near an airfield at Hoernum on the island of Sylt in North Germany.

Jones took his findings to the RAF and to Professor Lindemann, Prime Minister Churchill's scientific adviser. He attended a high defense meeting and told his story, and although most of the officials were skeptical, Churchill told him to pursue the subject.

The RAF appointed an air marshal to supervise the research, and a squadron of aircraft with specially fitted planes to try to locate the beams. Soon he had located beams at Schleswig-Holstein and at Cleve, which were set to intersect over England.

Soon the RAf squadron reported back that a plane taking off from Wyton airfield and flying north had encountered the beam, a narrow beam about five hundred yards wide passing through a certain position. So all doubts were removed and the RAF set out first to jam the beams and make them unusable to the Germans.

On June 27 Dr. Jones was shown another Enigma German secret message.

IT IS PROPOSED TO SET UP KNICKEBEIN AND WOTAN INSTALLATIONS NEAR CHERBOURG AND BREST.

In the course of this investigation, Dr. Jones also learned of the existence of the German Freya air defense apparatus and that there were stations near Cherbourg and Brest, that they had detected the destroyer *Delight* at a range of sixty miles, and that the Luftwaffe had then found and sunk her on July 29 as a part of the preliminary Battle of Britain campaign.

But Knickebein did not emerge as a major threat in these early days of the battle, and so some at the Air Ministry and in the RAF dismissed the whole matter as foolish.

Still, on July 27 a document was recovered from a German bomber which reported that to use Knickebein at long range, the aircraft receivers were to be tuned up by special squads, whose services would be made available on request. On July 27 Enigma reported that a *Kampf Geschwader* No. 54 had requested such a tune-up for its three squadrons, each of twenty-seven bombers. This was to happen in the week of August 5.

Since this *Geschwader* was to operate in west England, Dr. Jones knew then that the Cherbourg Knickebein would begin operating sometime in early August.

The day air battle had begun on July 10, and on July 12 had switched to radar stations and airdromes. Dr. Jones was expecting night attacks to start at any time, and on August 23 he watched a night attack on Birmingham. It seemed to him that Knickebein must be coming very soon.

# CHAPTER 6

# *The Air Struggle Begins*

All that had gone before was preliminary. Britain now faced the decisive struggle. If Hitler was to invade the British Isles, he had to have control of British skies. As Prime Minister Churchill put it:

> Our fate now depended upon victory in the air. The German leaders had recognized that all their plans for the invasion of Britain depended on winning air supremacy above the Channel and the chosen landing places on our south coast. The preparation of the embarkation ports, the assembly of the transports, the minesweeping of the passages, and the laying of new minefields were impossible without protection from British air attack. For the actual crossing and landings, complete mastery of the air over the transports and the beaches was the decisive condition. The result, therefore, turned upon the destruction of the Royal Air Force and the system of airfields between London and the sea.

Hitler had told Admiral Raeder (although the British did not then know it) that unless Marshal Goering's Luftwaffe could gain control of the air in eight days, he would delay the invasion of England until the following spring.

Admirals Raeder and Doenitz lamented the Führer's sense

of priority. They thought, first should be the naval targets, and the Luftwaffe should have been pasting such targets for weeks. What the navy men did not understand was the need for the Luftwaffe to recuperate from the battle for France, in which they had lost many aircraft and their organization had been hit by losses of key commanders. But the Luftwaffe was given very little time by Hitler, or by Goering, who even now seemed to be growing away from the understanding of the problems of the air force he had created. When informed that the Luftwaffe had gathered only 2,669 operational aircraft for the coming operations—only 1,015 bombers, 346 dive-bombers, 933 fighters, and 375 heavy fighters—Goering turned sadly to an aide.

"And this is my Luftwaffe?" he sighed.

It was, and within the perameters of its degree of rebuilding, that Luftwaffe was ready to undertake the destruction of the RAF, and confident that it would be able to accomplish the task in short order.

From the French airfields, the aircraft of the Luftwaffe's *Luftflotte* 1 and *Luftflotte* 2 began sending this armada toward England, beginning before dawn on August 13, *Adlertag*. The first wave consisted of seventy-four Dornier bombers stationed at three airfields. To accompany them were several score of the twin-engined Me-110 fighter planes. They made rendezvous, the fighters and the bombers, over Amiens, whence they were to make the crossing of the Channel at twelve thousand feet. But suddenly at a little past six o'clock that morning, the whole operation was scrubbed. Marshal Goering, who had been up early and was excited to participate in the first day of the wrecking of English air power, had been informed that cloud cover over England was several thousand feet high and scarcely broken anywhere. Rather than risk the disgrace of failure on this first day, Goering had called the attack back. But although the fighter squadrons got the word, the bombers did not, and they proceeded, without fighter support, toward the Thames and their targets. They flew up the Thames Estuary, unnoticed in the heavy weather and undetected by the battered radar stations at Foreness, Dover, and Whitstable. A few miles northwest of Margate, one group of bombers peeled off to attack the naval base at Sheerness, while another headed toward Eastchurch.

But where were the German fighters to protect them? No one knew. This suddenly became a matter of importance when the RAF Spitfires and Hurricanes of three squadrons swooped in to attack. First to fall was a Dornier under the guns of Squadron Commander A. G. Malan. Then the Spitfires and Hurricanes were among the bombers, and the dogfights began. Some of the British fighters carried eight machine guns. Some of them carried twenty-millimeter cannon, which were more effective at long range. Another Dornier fell, this one to cannon fire, but then the range shortened, and the Dornier's gunners began to score. A Spitfire went down in flames, and another, with the pilot bailing out of the second and the parachute blossoming as it skirted the clouds.

Soon five Dorniers had been destroyed and another six damaged, one so badly that it crash-landed in Kent, with four of the crew surviving to become prisoners of war.

This first raid, then, was anything but a success, and when Goering learned of the muddle that had sent the Dorniers over England without their fighter escort, he was furious.

The second effort was to be made by *Luftflotte* 3 later in that afternoon, from the French airfields farther west and south than those of *Luftflotte* 2. First the Luftwaffe sent over a number of Me-109s, to rouse up the British fighters, and hopefully to involve them in aerial jousting while the bombers got through. But the British of fighter command were too canny, and they only sent up one squadron of Spitfires to deal with the invading Me-109s, and kept the rest on the ground awaiting the word as to whence the real bomber attack would come.

The major attack was from the west, assembling over the Cherbourg peninsula, and it consisted of Ju-88 bombers and Stuka dive-bombers, escorted by Me-109s and Me-110s. About three hundred planes were involved, and they were heading for southern England, around Southampton, but with orders to concentrate on the British airfields and the fighter defenses.

As the Germans approached the coast, the radar detected them and two squadrons of Hurricanes were sent out to deal with them. They were outnumbered at least ten to one, but they moved in to attack, skirting around the bombers, and avoiding their gunners as much as possible. It was shortly after 4:00 P.M. that the action began, and soon it was moving over Southampton, which was the target of many of the attacking bombers, using high explosives and incendiaries, on the town and on the docks. Among the obvious targets was the Spitfire factory there, but it was scarcely damaged.

By four o'clock that afternoon, all of the fighters of Air Group 10 were in the air. The action became confused as the German squadrons broke up to deal with various targets assigned to them. The Germans were hampered by scattered cloud and poor visibility, and several squadrons poured their bombs across the countryside, hitting nothing in particular. The air station at Middle Wallop was one of the primary targets assigned to two squadrons of Ju-88s, but in the bad weather they failed to find the target, and instead of hitting this primary field, they wasted their bombs on an auxiliary field miles away near Andover. Another squadron of Stukas, escorted by Me-109s, suddenly found that its escort had disappeared and been replaced by a squadron of Spitfires. This was Squadron 609, which got between the German fighters and the slow Stukas, and began shooting. Some of the British fighters engaged the Me-109s, and one was shot down from an altitude of fifteen thousand feet. Six Ju-87 Stukas were shot down at this time, too.

In the afternoon the Germans were back again, this time attacking Rochester and Detling fields near Maidstone. This was to be a sort of coup de main for the Luftwaffe, and Marshal Kesselring had been misinformed that the fields hit the day before and the radar installations had been permanently disabled. Thus he believed that with the smashing of these three, he would open a clear field for German bombing of the military targets and also clear the way for the invasion, if that would still be necessary.

Again the attack was made with the dive-bombers, and again they proved inadequate for the job, too slow, too vulnerable, and because of the weather, too prone to get lost. This group did get lost, they did not find their targets, and were intercepted by British fighters. The group destined for Rochester got scattered all over southern England; some were shot down, and the others jettisoned their bombs and headed home to friendlier French airfields.

Detling Aerodrome near the Thames Estuary stood out like a mountain on the southern English countryside, with its three big hangars and many smaller buildings clustered around the runways. It was a part of RAF coastal command, not of fighter command, and thus was not hooked up to Air Marshal Dowding's alert system. Forty Stukas, escorted by Me-109s, left the French fields to attack this target, and found it without fail. They passed over Maidstone and Chatham, and the air raid warning radar found them and began tracking, but they came on inexorably. There was plenty of warning for the airmen of the RAF, but their station commander chose not to heed it. The air raid sirens blaring in Chatham and Maidstone were quite apparent at Detling, but life went on there as usual, because the commander had ordained that no attention was to be paid to air raids elsewhere, and only if the field itself was about to come under attack would defensive measures be invoked.

When the attack was imminent, the men on the ground had about ten seconds to invoke their defenses. The surprise was complete; most of the airmen were on their way to afternoon tea in messes when they heard, not their own sirens, but the sound of many airplane engines, and looking up, they saw scores of Me-109s peeling off and diving on the field to strafe. They scattered and ran, as the Stuka dive-bombers broke out of the cloud cover above and began their deadly work.

The airmen ran toward the bomb shelters, but many of them never made it, and some who did make it were unlucky enough to dive into shelters that were struck by bombs, so that seventy of them died, including the station commander, whose carelessness had caused the problem. He was killed, along with several of his officers, at the entrance to his headquarters.

On the field, the station's Blenheim fighter bombers, loaded with fuel and bombs for a mission against the French ports where invasion barges had been spotted, were a primary target of the attack, and soon they began exploding and the flames spreading to others.

In all, twenty-two aircraft were destroyed, and so were two of the hangars, plus many stores, fuel, and ammunition in storage. The destruction was so complete that Field Marshal Kesselring reported to Goering that this particular station had been knocked out for good. He also reported that no aircraft had been lost on the raid on Detling Aerodrome.

Goering also learned that night, however, successes in the other raids on Southampton, Portland, the airfields at Andover, Eastchurch, and Lympne and in night raids on the aircraft factories at Birmingham and Belfast. Five of the new Stirling heavy bombers were destroyed at Belfast, but relatively little hurt was suffered at Birmingham, even though four bombers dropped their explosives there. In the day's fighting, Goering learned, the Luftwaffe had lost forty-five aircraft. The commanders claimed to have shot down several score of British planes, but the actual loss to the RAF that day was thirteen fighters.

Prime Minister Churchill had decided that it was high time to carry the war to the Italians, to teach them that their jackal approach would have its price, and that night of August 13 the RAF sent thirty-six Whitley bombers off to bomb Milan and Turin. They had to carry more fuel than bombs for the long journey across the Alps, and so the raid was more symbolic than effective, but its effect was profound nonetheless. The Italians expressed great outrage that their air space had been violated, although the damage was minimal.

August 14 dawned cloudy, but as the day wore on, the clouds cleared from time to time over much of England, and the flying weather was more than adequate for another Luftwaffe attack. But the morning fog and heavy cloud over France and England delayed the takeoffs. The Luftwaffe pilots began to learn of the heavy loss of Stukas the day before, and this news was not uplifting. But as the day brightened, they began to prepare for another assault, one to be carried out, however, on a much more restrained level than that of *Adlertag*. Luftwaffe enthusiasm remained at a high pitch. *Luftflotte* commanders Kesselring and Sperrle believed that most of the job had already been done in the last two days and that it was now a question of picking up the pieces and destroying what remained of the fragmented fighter command of Britain. So the Battle of Britain entered its second day.

# CHAPTER 7

# *Crucial Day*

On the night of *Adlertag*, Marshal Goering warned his *Luftflotte* commanders that their greatest effort must come on August 15. He and they believed that in the almost continuous air battles against the Kent area and the Channel coast, they had blunted Britain's air defenses, and they were now ready to make a major daylight raid to finish the job. Sperrle and Kesselring were told to keep the RAF occupied on August 14, so they would suspect nothing about the big plans for the fifteenth.

On that day, the fourteenth, King George VI went out to raise British morale by an inspection trip to the antiaircraft guns of Dartford and Welling. The king made an impressive figure in his ceremonial uniform and brought cheer with his good humor. If the morale of the Germans was high, then so was the morale of the British civilians and the soldier gunners. And so was the morale of the RAF, whose pilots were determined to weather the German storm.

To keep the British confused that day, General Sperrle mounted a series of three plane raids to keep the RAF occupied and off balance. It was impossible for the RAF to respond to every one of the raids, and some of them scored some successes. The major effort of Sperrle's *Luftflotte* was against Middle Wallop in Hampshire that day. Two squadrons of fighters were located at the field, and the pilots were very busy fending off attacks, attacking, and then landing amid the craters of their runways, to rearm and refuel and fight again. Dover and Sealand and Manston were also targets of the German attack, but no great damage was done, save to Middle Wallop, where a hangar was hit squarely by a five-hundred-pound bomb, doing considerable damage. That day, nineteen Luftwaffe planes were destroyed, as compared to eight British fighters, and the Germans lost one of their most skilled officers, Squadron Commander Alois Storckl, flying a Heinkel bomber that was shot down after bombing Middle Wallop, the plane crashing into the center of a naval ammunition dump near East Dean.

In spite of the excitement at Middle Wallop, the afternoon seemed to Air Marshal Dowding like a lull in the battle, and he had a hunch that the next day would see some unusual fireworks, particularly when the weather forecast that evening called for clear skies.

The Luftwaffe had decided to make a major air raid on the manufacturing cities in the north. The distance was too great for the Me-109s, so the fighter protection would all be the longer-range but slower Me-110s. The Luftwaffe chief of intelligence, Oberst Josef Schmidt, had been studying the disposition of British fighter squadrons in the past month and now convinced himself that the northeast was wide open.

So on the night of August 14, from Marshal Goering's headquarters went a radio message to General Hans-Juergen Stumpff, telling him to mount the attack from his *Luftflotte* 5. On that morning of August 15, about one hundred bombers with an escort of forty Me-110s were launched against the northern industrial area, while a raid of eight hundred Luftwaffe planes was sent against the south. The Germans were sure that all the available British fighters would be located in the south, and the northern attack would have good results.

But Air Chief Marshal Dowding had foreseen just such a possibility, and a few days earlier had relieved seven of his hard-pressed fighter squadrons from daily fighting in the south and moved them north, for a rest and to guard the industrial area against surprise attack.

The Germans came toward Newcastle upon Tyne in two large formations, one based in Norway and one in Denmark.

The Norway group was escorted by about twenty Me-110s, but the distance was so great that they had left their rear gunners behind and carried more gasoline than ammunition and bombs. The He-111 bombers carried sharply reduced bombloads.

The Germans complicated matters by making their landfall seventy-five miles too far north, which was an area where a feinting force of Heinkel seaplanes had been sent to draw off British firepower. Instead the British fighters moved out to meet the real attack force, because of the navigational error. Up in Yorkshire at lunchtime, Squadron 616's pilots were assembled at 12:40 and waiting to top off their lunch with a sweet when the order came to scramble. The pilots raced to the flight line, where the ground crews already had the aircraft ready for them with engines started. They jumped into their planes and took off, not knowing where they were going but instructed to fly out to sea. In ragged little batches, they had reached twelve thousand feet and Flamborough Head when they began to spot the enemy. First they saw a mass of small black dots, which grew in size until they could recognize about sixty Ju-88 bombers, flying in formation, but without fighter escort. The Spitfires of Squadron 616 moved in to attack, supported by some Hurricanes of Squadron 73, which had also been scrambled.

In short order the British fighters downed seven of the Ju-88s. Three more, heading back across the North Sea to their Scandinavian bases, were so badly damaged that they crash-landed on the enemy side. These were planes of KGr 30, which was based at Aalborg, Denmark. The surviving bombers pressed on toward Tyneside, beginning to encounter heavy antiaircraft fire, which disposed of another Ju-88. Others bombed the airfield at Driffield, north of Hull, thinking it was a fighter field, and destroyed ten bombers in four of the field's ten hangars. But that was their only success. The planes of *Luftflotte 5* suddenly encountered not two fighter squadrons but six, and most of the pilots were highly experienced in the recent battles, men who had been sent to the north "for a rest."

Soon four British fighter squadrons were engaging the German enemy, and seven Me-110s were shot down in short

order. The surviving Luftwaffe fighters sought the cover of
the clouds, and the British fighters, Spitfires and Hurricanes,
concentrated on the Heinkel bombers. With quick attacks,
they split up formations, and the Heinkels began to falter,
some of them jettisoning their bombs across the countryside
from Sunderland to Newcastle. Soon the straggling bombers
headed back across the North Sea, their mission in shambles.
Not a single British fighter was shot down, although the
Luftwaffe claimed eleven kills.

By one o'clock in the afternoon the battle was raging, and
half an hour later it was all over and the British pilots were
landing at their airfields and telling their stories to the intelligence officers.

On the other side, the commanders of the *Luftflotte* were
summoned to Karinhall, the country mansion of Marshal
Goering, to explain what was going wrong with the marshal's
foolproof plan to bring Britain to its knees with his "Eagle
attack." But that day the assault continued in the south, with
two groups of Stuka Ju-87s attacking the airfields at Hawkinge
and Lympne once again, although their superiors claimed to
Goering that the fields had been destroyed in the earlier raids.
The bombers were accompanied by Me-109s.

The first assault on the South that day was launched just
before eleven in the morning. From airfields in the interior,
thirty bombers took off, followed by forty more a few minutes
later and then by sixty more from fields near the coast at
11:35 A.M. Half of these flights headed straight across the
Channel for Lympne, Hawkinge, and West Malling, but the
other half flew up the Thames Estuary past Manston and
Eastchurch.

The Germans met their fighters and then crossed the Channel. They ran into three squadrons of Hurricanes and two
squadrons of Spitfires, which broke up the attack on Hawkinge, shooting down two bombers and damaging others,
until the Me-109s descended from on high and shot down
four British fighters. At Lympne the Luftwaffe had better
luck, the bombers escaping notice and making their bomb
runs without interception. Meanwhile the fighter bombers and
fighters nearer the French coast were preparing a surprise for
the British. Later that afternoon a group of Me-110s and Me-

109s raided Manston, coming in from low level, and Martlesham Heath, carrying five-hundred- and one-thousand-pound bombs. At the latter station they did considerable damage, wrecking two hangars and destroying many stores, and a Fairey bomber all loaded for an attack on the invasion barges on the French coast.

Still later, another attack was launched from the airfields farther west in France, well on the west side of the Seine River and on the Normandy peninsula.

This attack involved some three-hundred German aircraft in a number of small raids in the Portland and Southampton area, on the ports and on the airfields. This was the heaviest German raid to date, and the British put up 150 fighters from fourteen squadrons to meet it. The action began at about four o'clock in the afternoon. The fighter controller calmly told one flight of five Hurricanes to be prepared to meet ninety enemy planes twenty miles south of Portland at 29,000 feet. Then he came on the air a moment later.

"Sorry about that," he said. "Its a hundred and twenty aircraft at eighteen thousand."

The Hurricanes fanned out to search, and a few minutes later one of them made the first sighting, a mass of black dots dead ahead. As the dots separated into shapes, they became a horde of Ju-87s supported by fighters above, in tight formations at fourteen-thousand feet and up. The Hurricanes headed straight in. Squadron Leader Ian Gleed of Squadron 87 led his four pilots in, opening fire as soon as he came within range of the tightly packed Stukas. Then the Me-109s sliced down, and the melee became general. Flight officer Roland Beemont found an Me-110 firing on him from front and below. He dove down, and shot down the German fighter, but was immediately attacked by another. The odds were more than ten to one in favor of the Germans, but the RAF pilots had the satisfaction of having plenty of targets. In this fight, one of the five Hurricanes was shot down and splashed in the Channel, but the pilot was later rescued.

Twelve of the fourteen British fighter squadrons engaged the enemy that afternoon, the other two squadrons somehow failed to find the Germans. Many British pilots were shot down, wounded, and crawled out of their wrecked aircraft to go and fight again. Some were captured by ground personnel and loaded into ambulances, but the wounded airmen tended to escape at the hospital and re-join their squadrons if they could still walk.

Other pilots that afternoon landed their planes and emerged from aircraft so smashed up that they would not fly again, some of the airmen without a scratch on them. One pilot, wounded in action over the Channel, became disoriented and landed in France, to be captured by the Wehrmacht. Another shot down three Germans, but landed at Manson Field during a bombing raid, and was very nearly bombed out, then attacked on the field by a strafing Me-110, and shot at by his own antiaircraft guns. Late in the afternoon he was attacked and the plane disabled so that he bailed out, and parachuted safely.

In the middle of the afternoon 90 Dornier bombers escorted by 130 Me-109s were spotted by the Dover radar. Three squadrons of Britain's Air Group 11 came up to meet them. Squadron 151 lost six Hurricanes in a hurry, shot down or badly damaged. The bomber group split over the land, and half headed for Eastchurch and half to Rochester, to strike two aircraft factories, which they thought were producing fighter planes. The fact was that these factories were producing bombers, not fighters, but the damage done to them was severe and set back production for several weeks.

The final assault on August 15 began at six P.M. on this long summer evening, with the Germans taking off from western French fields to assault the airfields at Biggin Hill and Kenley. A force of Dorniers came first, after a fighter sweep of Me-109s. The famous German bombing squadron Erpro 210 led the attack, its second of the day, with fifteen Me-110 fighter bombers and eight Me-109s. But the 110s failed to make contact with their 109 escort, but kept on toward Kenley, to pave the way for the Dornier bombers. When they got to the airfield they met fighters, but they were not German fighters, but British—Hurricanes of Squadron 111. Nine planes had been scrambled from Croydon airfield, and they had climbed to ten thousand feet to await their enemies. The Germans were aiming for Kenley, which was outside the Greater London circle, but the Hurricanes jumped them over Croydon, which was inside that circle, and the Germans dropped their bombs in a hurry. One could hardly say that the bombs were aimed, but rather jettisoned; still they did damage, knocked out a Hurricane repair plant, several hangars, and the terminal building of the Croydon passenger airport. Then the British fighters pounced, and the Me-109s, with limited fuel, made a few passes and then fled for the French coast and safety. The slower Me-110s were now outnumbered by more fighters, a squadron of Hurricanes from Biggin Hill having joined the fight, and six 110s and one Me-109 were shot down.

Prime Minister Winston Churchill had held a cabinet meeting at No. 10 Downing Street that morning, and after the meeting, he had left to visit fighter command headquarters and find out how the air battle was progressing. Earlier Churchill had often been critical of Air Marshal Dowding, particularly in Dowding's refusal to send fighters to help the French, which had seriously embarrassed Churchill with French Premier Paul Reynaud and caused much suspicion (well founded) by the French of British intentions in the last days of the French campaign; now Churchill was eloquent in his praise of the stubborn air marshal's policy. Indeed, that day it may have saved Britain's air strength in the face of this mighty challenge.

Altogether, the air battle raged across a front of five hundred miles, with five major actions fought. The Germans had sent over 1,750 sorties, missed most of the targets at which they aimed, and violated the area of Greater London, which Hitler had said should not be hit, because he still had hope of persuading the British to come to an ''accommodation'' with him. Still that night he made the final preparations for the invasion of Britain, scheduling the date for September 15, presupposing that Marshal Goering's Luftwaffe would have lived up to the marshal's promises.

In the south all twenty-two of the fighter squadrons were engaged, some of them as many as three times during the day. The squadrons of fighter command had flown 974 sorties during the day. The German losses for the day were seventy-five planes to the British thirty-four.

Goering had boasted that his Luftwaffe would destroy Britain's air might in four days. Three days of that time had now passed, and when his *Luftflotte* chiefs returned to their commands after the meeting at Karinhall that night, they had very little to say. No one had argued against Goering's command that they stop wasting their time hitting the British radar stations, and concentrate on the airfields. It was the greatest error of Goering's career so far, and it turned the tide of the Battle of Britain. It was obvious to the chiefs, if not yet to Goering, that they were a long way from finishing the job. Both sides, however, were magnifying their victories and minimizing their losses. The British claimed many more planes shot down, 182, than was the actuality, probably 43. All this added to the British feeling of success in the battle, even though they did not know that it was in Goering's blunder they had been given back the key to victory.

The importance of the air battle of Britain was now known to all the world. Major Alexander P. DeSeversky, the advocate of air power as the key to victory in war, wrote in the New York *Times* that he agreed with Goering that if the Germans won the battle, they would have won the war and there would be no need for the invasion that Hitler was planning. The next few days would tell the tale.

# CHAPTER 8

# After Black Thursday, What?

Black Thursday was the name the Luftwaffe pilots gave to August 15 as they counted their heavy losses, which included Hauptmann Walter Rubensdoerffer, commander of Erpro 210, the crack Me-110 fighter bomber unit, who had crashed in the misdirected Croydon raid. Half a dozen other senior Luftwaffe pilots had also been lost that day.

Still, Air Marshal Goering was determined to persist in the raids against what he believed were the vital RAF airfields, on the theory that he would put them out of action and force the British back farther and farther from the coast and finally knock out fighter command. But, as noted, Goering erred badly in ordering the stoppage of the raids on the radar installations, perhaps because he did not completely understand their importance. Adolf Galland, who was to become Germany's premier fighter pilot, knew that somehow the British were controlling the activities of the airmen from the ground, because he could hear the commands of the fighter controllers, swift and accurate, directing the Spitfires and Hurricanes against the German formations. What he and the other pilots did not then know was that because of the radar, from the moment that the Luftwaffe planes took off from the French, Belgian, and other bases, they were spotted on the British radar screens and plotted so that they could be accurately attacked. It was thus that the British forces, heavily outnumbered, could meet their enemies on better than equal terms.

As Squadron Commander Peter Townsend put it:

"Ventnor had been wrecked in one attack. Half a dozen attacks on the four others already damaged would have wrecked them too."

All the stations were extremely vulnerable. Carpet bombing would have blown them sky-high because all the installations were in flimsy structures above ground. But the Germans never knew. Their intelligence officer said not to waste time on radar stations, they were no more important than Brighton Pier. One important Luftwaffe official said to forget the radar stations, because they would direct the British fighters to the German fighter formations, which would then shoot them down.

And Air Marshal Goering was obdurate. Forget the radar stations, he said. Concentrate on the airfields.

So the radar stations were ignored. And they continued to find the German enemy so the sector operations rooms could send the fighters out to find the Luftwaffe and inflict serious losses on his squadrons.

August 16 dawned, the skies over Britain and France filled with early morning mist, which prevented early flight operations. The Luftwaffe bomber squadrons were calling up reserves to replace the thirty-five crews lost on Black Thursday, and the air fleets dug into their reserves of aircraft. By nine o'clock the skies were clearing and the Luftwaffe operations began again. The first raid of the day was directed against the airfield at West Malling, and arrived shortly after 11:00 A.M. The radar scopes had not given a very good estimate of the size of the German force coming in, and so a minimal fighter force was scrambled, which was unable to contain the Dornier bombers. The uncompleted West Malling field was bombed and several new craters were opened on the runways and parking area.

Noon brought a big raid of three hundred planes, and the radar showed it accurately, so more than eighty fighters were put up to meet it. The first squadron to get into action was the Spitfire Squadron No. 54, which put up nine aircraft.

They bored in on the Dorniers, and soon the bombers were jettisoning their bombs over the countryside and streaking for home, showing the advantage of a quick attack pressed straight home. A few seconds later—actually—the Me-109 fighters from above were down on the Spitfires and the dog-fights began. But they did not last; the Me-109s did not have the range to stay around, and they could only fire a few bursts and then turn for the coast if they wished to make it back to their airfields. One pilot shot at two Me-109s. One of them crashed over England. The other managed to make the French coast, and crashed on its own airfield.

It was soon apparent that today's was to be another major effort. A vast horde of Dorniers flew over the English coast, and then split into small formations, each heading for a different airfield. Two Hurricane and three Spitfire squadrons met them and speared into the bomber formations, a line abreast, heading straight in. One fighter pilot misjudged the distance, held his attack on too long, and crashed into a Dornier, killing the British pilot and the German crew of four.

Over the Kent coast a fight developed between a squadron of Spitfires and a squadron of Me-109s, which saw one Me-109 shot down, but five Spitfires lost, while a little later in the day farther west, a new raid on the airfields, developed. The Germans were very skillful at timing; this new bombing raid against the airfields was scheduled to come in just as the first one had finished, a move designed to give the Germans the advantages of surprise when the RAF fighters were re-fueling and rearming after the first raid.

A group of Stukas headed for Tangmere Airfield, diving down from twelve-thousand feet, and several of them were jumped by Hurricane fighters, but the rest screamed down, the sirens invented by Ernst Udet screaming away and adding terror to the attack, at least theoretically. It was very difficult for the gunners at the antiaircraft guns to fire, because British fighters were taking off as the Germans came in, so the Germans achieved the surprise they wanted. Two of Tangmere's hangars were destroyed and three were damaged, with a loss of six Blenheim fighter bombers and seven Hurricanes on the ground.

But the Germans paid. They lost seven Stukas to the Hurricanes, and three more were damaged, and the antiaircraft guns shot down another Stuka over Tangmere Field. One Hurricane was lost.

In the fighting with the Me-109s and 110s, two Hurricanes were set afire and the pilots bailed out. As they drifted to earth, the antiaircraft gunners decided they were enemy and opened fire. They killed one of the British pilots and wounded the other.

Later that afternoon on Goering's orders, *Luftflotte* 2 and *Luftflotte* 3 sent more attacks from France and the low countries to the south and the area around London, although still respecting the London circle as inviolate. Late in the afternoon the good weather came to an end with thickening clouds all across the south of England. The change made it hard for the Germans to find their targets but equally hard for the radarmen, and the defenders had to depend on the reports from the Observer Corps. Many of the German planes flew over the British countryside undetected, searching for targets, attacking anything that looked like an airfield. As a result, several emergency airstrips were hard hit, but so were many airfields, and more aircraft were destroyed on the ground than in any other raid before this time.

Two JU-88s flew over a training field west of Oxford, undetected, and dropped their bombs on the hangar area. They destroyed nearly fifty training planes and eleven Hurricanes on the ground, then disappeared and were never found by the fighters.

But most of the German bombers that day failed to find their targets in the worsening weather, and so half a dozen major fighter fields, scheduled to be attacked, were untouched, and the bombers either dropped their loads on the countryside or took them home again. The results of the day were not very satisfactory for the Luftwaffe. They lost forty-five aircraft in the day and night raids, as opposed to the British loss of twenty-one fighters. But there were other losses that worried Prime Minister Churchill, particularly to bomber command, which saw twenty-eight bombers destroyed on the ground. These figures did not appear in the records of the

Battle of Britain, but they were real nonetheless, and a source of great concern to the War Cabinet.

August 17 was a day of respite. The Luftwaffe was moving in planes to replace the losses of the last few days, and virtually suspended operations, so the British did likewise. The day was spent at the British air stations in rebuilding and repairing, the demolition of wrecked hangars, and the filling in of bomb craters on the runways. Communications lines broken in the bombings were rebuilt, and tents were erected on some airfields to replace the bombed-out barracks. On others the personnel were quartered temporarily in houses nearby, most of which had been deserted by their civilian occupants with the coming of the air raids on the airfields.

On August 18 the Germans launched their most aggressive raiding yet, in their attempt to wipe out the southern airfields of the fighter command. Me-109s were first employed to make fighter sweeps and thus draw the British fighters up from the fields, whereupon the bombers and their escorts would come in to attack. This tactic had been decided by Goering in consultation with Field Marshal Kesselring. The difference this day was that the Luftwaffe concentrated on two targets, Kenley and Biggin Hill. The plans had been laid during the day of respite, and the crews were up before dawn for their briefings on the French airfields. The attacks were to begin with Stuka raids on the station buildings, followed by a high-level bombardment by Dornier bombers. Third would be a low-level attack, with the bombers coming in at treetop level, and thus evading the watchfulness of the British observers (and radar).

In fact, however, the German timing was off this day, and the squadron of Dornier bombers delegated to the low-level raid arrived first—not last, as had been expected. The British were waiting, the antiaircraft gunners at their guns, and the ground crews employing a new weapon, a length of heavy cable called Parachute and Cable—PAC. This weapon consisted of a length of steel cable launched by a rocket, which then blossomed forth with a parachute that suspended the cable as it descended slowly.

The Dorniers crossed the English coast without incident and roared over the countryside, frightening animals and people at an altitude of about one hundred feet off the ground. They evaded the radar by flying so low, but the Observer Corps caught them and reported, and soon enough the field at their target, Kenley, had the world that they were coming. But the British defenders did not expect the enemy aircraft to come in at so low a height, and they came in over the trees and began to bomb before a gun could be trained on them. They were carrying one-hundred-pound high-explosive antipersonnel bombs, and they deposited them quite accurately among the buildings of the air station. They bombed hangars, the administration building, messes, the operations room, and repair shops. Some bombs bounced down the runways, end over end, before exploding. Three hangars collapsed, and aircraft and gasoline began to explode. Kenley was a wreck. The attack was over in seconds, but the attackers had to get away, and as they sped across the field, the antiaircraft guns depressed and began to fire. At this range the machine guns were also effective, and one of them killed the pilot of one of the bombers, and one of the bombers struck one of the PAC cables that had just been launched, but bounced off and got away, but another Dornier struck a cable squarely and was brought down.

The German error in timing actually worked to the German advantage, because when the high-level and dive-bomber attackers arrived at the field, there was no mistaking it. The clouds of smoke arising from the devastated hangars and buildings were like a beacon in the English countryside.

The high-level bombers came next, Dorniers and Ju-88s, which bombed at twelve-thousand feet. They were pursued and attacked, along with their Me-110 escort, by several flights of Hurricanes. They were engaged by Me-110s, but the half dozen Hurricanes charged in among the fifty bombers and caused many of them to deviate from their bomb runs, and some of them to unload the bombs over the countryside. Another squadron of Hurricanes attacked the top cover of Me-109s, although the British fighters were outnumbered five to one. The problem here was the disparity in armament, the Me-109s carrying cannon, which were more effective than the Browning thirty-caliber machine guns, and so four Hurricanes were shot down in this attack.

The Ju-87s, the dive-bombers, seem to have gotten lost in this assault, but it was not necessary that they attack, because Kenley Airfield had been badly hurt. The station hospital had been destroyed, and a medical officer killed. The field's aircraft were advised to land at satellite fields. The water mains had been broken by the bombing, and so the fires burned for several hours until the civilian fire brigades arrived to help put out the flames. But by the end of the afternoon, communications had been restored and the airfield was again operational.

Biggin Hill, the second big air station on the Luftwaffe list for special attention that day, was attacked by some sixty He-111s and Ju-88s, with about fifty Me-109s on top for cover. A squadron of Spitfires came in to attack, accepting the odds of more than two to one. Here, as at Kenley, the low-level bombers arrived first, and the PAC rocket-chains went up, knocking two German bombers out. Two squadrons of British fighters were scrambled, and they shot down seven German aircraft from this attack.

Again the high-level bombers arrived at twelve-thousand feet, accompanied by Me-109 fighters, and again the British fighters went up to challenge them, causing some confusion in the bombing. Most of the bombs fell to the east of Biggin Hill Airfield and on the field, not on the all-important installations and hangars. The real danmage was caused by a group of Me-109s that came down to strafe the field just as planes of a Hurricane squadron were coming in to land and rearm. So many of this squadron's planes were destroyed that the unit was later withdrawn from the action until it could be rebuilt.

Over Ashford, at twenty-two thousand feet, a squadron of Hurricanes found five Me-110s and attacked, shooting them all down.

Later in the afternoon the Germans launched another major attack, this one on a coastal command airfield at Thorney Island and the naval air stations at Gosport and Ford, which had been touted by German air intelligence as very important installations. So important were they, the high command decided, that 111 dive-bombers were to be assigned to wiping them off the map, plus more than fifty Me-109s to provide air cover. At two o'clock in the afternoon this massive formation appeared over the Isle of Wight and headed east toward Portsmouth. The fighter control groups below scrambled several squadrons of British fighters, but it was hard for them to figure out where the enemy was going, and before anyone knew, twenty-odd bombers had hit Gosport, doing a lot of damage. The planes bound for Thorney Island, however, did not have so much luck. Two squadrons of British fighters got between them and their fighter protection and wrecked the neat formations, so that Thorney Island escaped much damage, but Poling and Ford did suffer, and the radar station at Poling was effectively knocked out of the battle, until after the end of August.

Was it worth the trouble? General Sperrle was not sure, for when his Stukas came home that afternoon, one Stuka Group was found to be almost totally disorganized. Its twenty-eight aircraft went out, but twelve failed to return and six others were so badly damaged that they barely made it back across the channel. In all that day, thirty Stukas were lost or so badly damaged as to be unusable. When the news reached Luftwaffe headquarters, the decision was made that the Stukas were no longer to be used in the Battle of Britain. They were too vulnerable.

At five-thirty that evening, another brilliant summer's ending, there were still three hours of daylight left when the Germans came in for another attack, this one on Essex, north of the Thames Estuary. More than one hundred Dornier bombers and Heinkels were heading for Hornchurch.

Most of the pilots of the nearby fighter fields had already flown two sorties that day, but it was time to scramble again, and they came up, the Hurricanes going after the bombers, and the Spitfires attacking the Me-109s.

Squadron Commander Peter Townsend of Squadron 85 at Debden was sent with his boys to patrol around Canterbury, and they took off a dozen Hurricanes strong. It was their job to go after the bombers, while the more maneuverable Spitfires tackled the Me-109s. Squadron 85 was in four sections that day. By this time the Hurricane pilots had learned how to deal with the Me-109s when jumped. The German plane, with its fuel injection, responded more quickly to emergency power than the Hurricane, but the Hurricane could outturn it, so when the Hurricane pilots got into trouble, they turned and turned and turned, did not climb, did not dive, if they wanted to stay alive.

This day Squadron 85 flew at ten thousand feet in cloud, over the Thames Estuary, and there saw "a massive column about a mile and a half high, stepped up wave upon wave. At the base were the Ju-87s, above them the Heinkels, then Dorniers and then Ju-88s. Then a layer of Me-110s, and at the top at twenty thousand feet, a whole nest of Me-109s."

The Hurricanes closed on the bombers and the Ju-87s, and the Heinkels turned back toward the sea, while a group of 110s formed around them for protection. The Hurricanes dashed in, knocking down several Me-110s, but then the 109s entered the fight. Townsend was attacked by a 109, turned, fired, and shot it down. He chased more Me-109s, but he could not catch the faster German planes. He ran out of ammunition and headed back to his base at Debden. When he arrived, he found two of his pilots missing. One of them came back. The other, who had lost his head in the chase and followed an Me-109 out to sea, against better judgment, did not come back.

Other British fighters were also mixing it up with the enemy. One pilot single-handedly headed into a group of fifty bombers, and broke up their formation before he was jumped by half a dozen Me-109s and shot down. Then into the fighting came two of the intrepid Polish pilots of Squadron 501. Among the fighters for England in the Battle of Britain were representatives of more than a dozen nations, Americans, Canadians, Australians, New Zealanders, South Africans, Rhodesians, Jamaicans, Irishmen, Czechs, Belgians, Frenchmen, Palestinians, and Poles. The fliers from the countries overrun by Germany had a double stake in the battle, and among them the Czechs and the Poles were the fiercest in their hatred of the Germans. They were seeking more than victory, but revenge for what the enemy had done to their countries, and sometimes to their friends and relatives and loved ones. This afternoon these two Polish pilots in short order shot down an Me-109 each, one of which was piloted by Hauptmann Horst Tietzen, one of the most prominent "aces" of the German fighting force.

The fight lasted for half an hour, and then the skies quieted down after what the pilots of fighter command called the hardest day of the battle. But while the Germans straggled, they did damage. The weather began to close in, and the bombers searched for targets they could not find and then dropped their bombs, often on civilian targets. So Black Thursday was followed by Bloody Sunday, as the Battle of Britain went on.

That night Luftwaffe Intelligence Officer Beppo Schmidt reported to Goering that it had cost ten bombers to wipe out Kenley, which he had crossed off the fighting map. No more, said Goering. It was not worth it, no more low-level raids. And so Goering eliminated the Luftwaffe's last chance of wiping out the radar eyes of fighter control.

# CHAPTER 9

# *"The Decisive Phase . . ."—Goering*

On August 19 Reichsmarschal Goering called his Luftwaffe leaders to another conference at Karinhall. It began at noon, with a blast from the commander of the Luftwaffe, delivered in stony tones.

"I am not at all pleased with the way this battle is going. It should have been finished in a few days, but serious errors have led to unnecessary losses."

As to the Ju-87 Stukas, he accepted the verdict that they should be withdrawn from the battle, but the fault, he said, lay with the fighters for not giving them adequate protection. Field Marshal Milch, the inspector general, defended the fighters and laid the blame squarely at the feet of Goering's staff. It was the fault of the high command, he said; they had issued the wrong orders, sending the Stukas to do jobs they could not do.

Goering summarized the situation. They were, he said, in the decisive phase of the battle against England, and everything in the future depended on what the Luftwaffe did now. They absolutely had to break the strength of the RAF fighter command. To do that, they had to lure the fighters up into the air, not try to destroy them on the ground. They should schedule their bombing raids within easy range of the fighter bases.

Goering's belief was based on information from intelligence officer Beppo Schmidt, whose understanding of the actual situation was faulty. The RAF knew that the Germans had a good chance of beating them if they could keep the pressure on the airfields, destroying planes on the ground. But the reports that came in from the squadrons were wildly inflated; on the eighteenth alone, the Luftwaffe claimed to have destroyed 134 British fighters, when the actual score was 27. The Luftwaffe believed that the way to defeat the British was to engage them in combat; when fighter command knew—as it has seen with such trepidation—that if the Germans knocked out the radar stations and the operations rooms, and cut communications, it did not make any difference how many fighters Britain put up, no one would be able to tell them where to go to find the enemy.

Goering now rearranged the priorities and tasks. From now on, *Luftflotte* 2, in the low countries and northern France, would attack by day. *Luftflotte* 31 would make night attacks, starting with Liverpool, and *Luftflotte* 5 in Scandinavia would make night attacks on Glasgow.

"The cloudy conditions likely to prevail over England in the next few days must be exploited for aircraft factory attacks. We must succeed in seriously disrupting the material supplies of the enemy Air Force by the destruction of its relatively small number of aircraft engine and aluminum plants. These attacks on enemy aircraft industry are of particular importance, and should also be carried out at night."

So Goering gave the orders that were to change the nature of the air war. He said that he would make the decisions about the bombing of cities (an usurpation of a power that Hitler had arrogated to himself).

Goering then kept his fighter leaders, Werner Moelders, his leading fighter ace, and Adolf Galland, who would later hold that honor, and lambasted them for the inefficiency of the German fighter operation. His answer was to promote these men, both in their late twenties, to become group leaders.

On the other side of the English Channel, Air Chief Marshal

Dowding was also making some estimates and changes. He calculated that since August 8, fighter command had lost 175 aircraft although the Germans claimed at least three times as many, and that he still had plenty of reserves, although the Germans thought he was scraping the bottom of the barrel. The fact was that aircraft production in Britain was increasing very nicely in spite of the attrition of bombing, largely because Lord Beaverbrook, the publisher turned aircraft production minister, had done a fine job of cutting through red tape and rearranging production priorities. Fighter production was about to hit five-hundred a month.

But Dowding's big worry just now was loss of personnel. He had lost ninety-four pilots killed and sixty wounded in ten days of fighting. What could be done? For one thing, unnecessary risks were not to be taken. That meant that there would be no more wild chases of German planes across the Channel. The British fighters would stay on their own side, or at least within easy gliding distance of the shore, so that if they were shot down, they would come home and not end up in a German prison camp.

For another, it was time to accept some volunteers, of which there were plenty. But the volunteers had to be skilled men, so they were the ones from the light bomber squadrons. After a week of training, fifty of them joined the fighter command squadrons. In the last ten days the destruction of air facilities had been greater than Dowding liked to contemplate. Six of his main radar stations had been hit, and two were out of commission, their areas covered by mobile sets. Three sector stations had been hit, and they were very vulnerable because they were above ground not below.

Churchill was concerned, particularly about the defeatist attitude shown in America. This attitude was fueled by Ambassador Joseph Kennedy's belief that the British were finished, and it was just a matter of time. The American newspapers sounded a note of gloom, and the reports were tinged with indications that the Germans were winning the battle.

"The important thing," Churchill said, "is to bring the German aircraft down and to win the battle, and the rate at which the American correspondents and the American public are convinced that we are winning, and that our figures are true, stands at a much lower level. They will find out quite soon enough when the German air attack is plainly shown to have been repulsed . . . We can, I think, afford to be a bit cool and calm about all this [although] I must say that I am a little impatient about the American skepticism. The event is what will decide all.''

In that, at least, Churchill agreed with Goering, who also was impatient for signs of victory. After his Luftwaffe leaders had left Karinhall, he thought about the battle and then issued new orders. The Luftwaffe must continue the fight against the British air force, he said, with the aim of weakening British fighter strength. The enemy was to be forced to bring his fighter formations into operation.

Since the British fighter formations were in operation day after day, this seemed to be an odd attitude, but Goering had the feeling that the British were holding something back. In fact, they were not, but ascending British fighter production may have made it seem that way.

It was decided at Karinhall, then, that the Ju-87 Stukas would be conserved for the invasion of Britain, except for two units, which would be held in reserve for sudden opportunities, like the chance to attack a big convoy.

The second change, not anticipated in the beginning, was that only one commissioned officer would be among the crew of a bomber, a change coming from the news that 136 Luftwaffe officers had been killed in the last ten days.

Another change was in the use of the Me-110, which had been found to be too vulnerable for fighter work. In the future it was to be used only when missions went beyond the range of the Me-109.

And it was reconfirmed that no more time or energy would be wasted on attacks on the British radar stations.

Finally Goering reaffirmed that the main effort would continue to be against the British fighters, concentration on the big airfields and on the British aircraft industry. In these attacks, the bombers flying over Britain would have more Me-109 protection.

On August 20 the weather dawned foul on both sides of the Channel, so air activity was restricted. The Germans lost seven aircraft that day, and the British two. The memorable event of the day was Prime Minister Churchill's speech to the House of Commons, in which he gave praise to the brave men of the RAF fighter command. "Never in the field of human conflict was so much owed by so many to so few . . ." he said, and all the world heard, and much of the world marveled at the bravery of this little band of men of all nations who were fighting the German enemy.

The next three days were also marked by weather so bad that aerial operations were very difficult. Goering made a trip on August 21 to Kesselring's *Luftflotte* 2 advanced headquarters at Cap Blanc Nez. Using high-power binoculars, he gazed across at the radar station at Dover, and watched the long-range coastal guns shelling Dover. The shelling was not very accurate.

The German losses for the three days were limited to nineteen aircraft, and British to six—in fact, on August 23 the British lost no planes at all. But there was activity, some of it awesome. On August 19 a formation of one hundred Me-109s swept along the south coast of England, trying to bring up fighters, as Goering had ordered them to do, but the British ignored them. "We want to shoot down bombers, not fighters" was the word from fighter control. Later that day, bombers attacked Southampton and Pembroke, hitting for the docks. The Germans raided the airfields of the south with fighter sweeps, and that was about all except for some strikes against convoys at sea, and a few bombs dropped at night, and not very effectually.

In this period of lull, the RAF also appraised the air war.

On virtually every occasion that the Germans operated in force they grossly outnumbered the defending squadrons. There were not sufficient forces available for a reserve of fighters . . . to be kept back and used only when the direction and strength of the enemy's attack were known. Instead the concentrated formations of German fighters and bombers were being met by squadrons containing no more than twelve and frequently fewer aircraft. It was rarely, therefore, that the Germans failed to reach their targets, provided that the state of the weather was fair. Nor is the relative strength of the opposing forces employed in one operation an adequate gauge of the odds involved. For whereas as many as seventy or eighty British fighters might engage enemy formations totalling anything from one hundred to three hundred aircraft, the individual fighter squadrons, since they normally came into action independently of each other, were engaging up to ten times their number of the enemy.

One reason that the Luftwaffe was still confident of victory was the state of reserves. They knew that they were wearing down the British fighter reserves. In fact, on August 9 there were 289 Spitfires and Hurricanes ready for action but not in action. One August 16 there were 235 reserves, and on August 23 there would be 161.

Finishing the assessment, the RAF Narrative of Battle said that there was so far no indication of victory for either side, but that "the Luftwaffe had suffered more severely than fighter command, and that it had not obtained a sufficient return in targets damaged or destroyed to compensate for its losses. On the other hand, it had so far used barely one-third of its available strength in the west. Fighter command for its part had lost pilots it could ill afford to lose; and the grim prospect of the fighter force slowly wasting away through lack of pilots was already apparent.

On August 24 the skies cleared. The first German raid of the day was launched on Great Yarmouth. Then the radarmen spotted what they had been waiting for, a great buildup over the Pas de Calais area. So the Germans were coming again, this time to Manston, North Weald, and Hornchurch as Marshal Kesselring tried to carry out Goering's orders to plaster the airfields. As his bombers finished, General Sperrle's came in. At about 3:45 in the afternoon the buildup was seen over Cherbourg and the bomber force and its fighters headed north toward St. Catherine's Point.

Things did not go well for the British that afternoon. The damage done to Ventnor radar station, prevented it from working very efficiently. What was reported as a single formation of German planes turned out to be at least seven medium-sized forces, but only one of them was a bomber formation. The fighters went up to meet them, but the information was faulty and they found themselves five thousand feet below the enemy planes, in the midst of their own British antiaircraft fire. Then the Me-109s swooped down . . .

There was very little the outclassed fighters could do to stop the raid that was on Portsmouth. More than two hundred 500-pound bombs were dropped on the naval installations and the streets of the town. The casualties were the highest of those of ground personnel in the battle so far, one hundred killed and three hundred wounded. And that night for the first time since the 1914-1918 war, bombs fell on the city of London. The plan now was for the Luftwaffe to send more than a thousand sorties per day over Britain, to knock the English out in a hurry. These bombs dropped on London were jettisoned, and were not intended to signal any change in German strategy, but the people affected could not be expected to know that.

On August 24 the Germans hit Manston for the last time, and the Ju-88s left the field a twisted mass of broken aircraft and broken burning buildings. Bombs severed the communications circuits, and the evacuation of the field was ordered.

Later in the afternoon the Germans hit North Weald and wrecked the powerhouse and caused a number of casualties. Next day, August 25, the Germans were back in the morning over the airfields, and they came all day long, losing twenty planes to the British sixteen.

After the accidental bombing of London the night before, Marshal Goering demanded to know who was responsible, and said he would be transferred to the infantry. But the damage was done, the bombing of London had begun, and that morning the War Cabinet met in London to talk about revenge. Prime Minister Churchill was in a vengeful mood, and so were the others.

British bombers had been hitting Germany all along, but the targets had been industrial zones in the Ruhr. Berlin, five hundred miles away, was untouched. But that night of August 25, eighty-one British bombers were sent to Berlin, to teach Hitler that he must take the consequences of bombing London. Until this point, the people of Berlin had scarcely known that a war was raging. They read their newspapers, but there were no signs of trouble at home.

They were sure, they had won the war. Only England held out, and everyone was certain that this would not last for long.

So when on the night of August 25 the air raid sirens began to wail, most people did not take them seriously. And instead of heading for the basements, they headed for the roofs to watch the show as the searchlights sought the tiny specks of planes in the sky.

The morning brought reports the British had bombed, and the bombs had fallen in residential and country areas.

On the morning of August 26 the Dorniers raided Debden sector station and did considerable damage. In the afternoon it was Portsmouth's turn again, but the next day it drizzled all day and operations were sharply curtailed, which gave the British a chance to shift fighter squadrons around.

That night the British were over Berlin again, and for the first time, Germans in the capital of the Third Reich were killed by enemies. The official count was ten killed and twenty-seven wounded. Next day the German press trumpeted stories of the "brutality" of the British. And the next night the British came again and the headlines read: BRITISH AIR PIRATES OVER BERLIN.

In a week of bombing, the British did not hit much, because the German Capital was defended by two rings of antiaircraft guns and hundreds of searchlight batteries. But the effect on the German people was electric. Suddenly they realized that the war was a serious matter. The first anniversary of the war was on them, and there was no peace in sight, nor any peace in sight as far as they could see.

On August 28 the Luftwaffe switched to heavier night raiding, as the Germans lost thirty aircraft and the British twenty. Next day the Germans tried the provocative fighter sweep again, but again without result as the British did not come up to challenge, but waited for the bombers. Kesselring claimed then that the Luftwaffe had accomplished its aim, and that fighter superiority had been established over England.

The words sounded good, and were given emphasis by very heavy bombing on the thirtieth and the thirty-first of the airfields and the area around Liverpool, especially at night.

So September came, and the RAF was growing worried, because the Germans did not seem to be affected by their losses and kept coming harder and harder. "Hammer at the enemy day and night to break his nerve," Goering had said. And the Luftwaffe was doing just that as September flew in.

The last two days of August, the Germans had mounted so many attacks that they had stretched the resources of fighter command to the breaking point. Field Marshal Kesselring had said he would stake his reputation on his ability to break the British before September 1. He sent over huge armadas of Me-109s, and when the British refused to rise to the bait, he made the bait sweeter by sending them again, this time escorting Ju-88s. He varied the timing of his raids, trying to catch the British fighters on the ground, rearming and re-gassing. Then he sent bomber formations of two hundred and more, which split up over southern England and attacked targets all over the south and east.

The British fighters responded with ever more daring tactics. The head-on attack became popular, which meant that the two aircraft would be coming at each other at a combined speed of six hundred miles an hour, or three hundred yards per second. As one pilot put it:

"The optimum range of our guns was about 300 yards, so if you could get your sights on at 600 yards, you could press the button for one second and that left you one second to break away."

One pilot who had heard about the tactic in the mess tried it out. He bored into a formation of He-111s and did not evade in time. His Hurricane bounced off the nose of a Heinkel bomber and both planes crashed. He parachuted to safety and suffered only a broken leg. In the hospital he complained, "I thought you told me they would break formation if we pressed home a good frontal attack."

"No," was the answer, "not if the pilot is dead."

"How do you know if he is dead or not?"

"The way you found out."

Sometimes the end was not quite so funny. Pilot Officer Percy Burton was hit and his plane began to trail smoke and flame. Others saw him straighten out and fly straight into a

German bomber; both crashed and Burton was killed. As the month of August ended, the German High Command was sensing victory. Major Freiherr von Falkenstein said that if they would only seize the opportunity of favorable weather to keep up the pressure, the victory was as good as won. And Air Chief Marshal Dowding was growing nervous because on August 31 his command lost thirty-nine planes, the highest figure yet. The Germans were still working over the fighter fields such as Hornchurch and Biggin Hill. In the first days of September the Germans concentrated on aircraft factories, with disturbing results. On September 4 a strong force of Me-110s was attacking the factory at Brooklands and was intercepted by nine Hurricanes, which shot down six of them in a few seconds and damaged another. But some of the bombers got through and hit the Vickets factory, causing seven hundred casualties. The destruction of a total of fifteen Me-110s still did not make up for this high casualty figure in an essential industry.

On September 5 several bombing raids escorted heavily by fighters were very effective, especially one against the Hawker factory at Brooklands. Every airfield in England was now feeling the pressure of the German attacks.

As Prime Minister Churchill said, there was great worry in the government. "In the fighting between August 24 and September 6, the scales had tilted against fighter command. During these crucial days the Germans had continually applied powerful forces against the airfields of the south and the southeast. Their object was to break down the day fighter defense of the capital, which they were impatient to attack."

Churchill saw the anxiety at Fighter Headquarters at Stanmore, and particularly at the headquarters of No. 11 Fighter Group at Uxbridge. Heavy damage had been done to five of the group's forward airfields and to six of their sector stations. Biggin Hill was so badly damaged that only one fighter squadron could operate from there for that last week. If the enemy had persisted in these attacks, the whole delicate organization of fighter command threatened to break down. But then on September 7 came a remarkable change in German direction.

# CHAPTER 10

# *The Bombing of London*

Beginning in July, the German navy had been assembling barges, steamers, tugs, and small boats along the coastal waters and moving them to the invasion ports. At the end of August, high-flying observation planes of the British Coastal Command had perceived a sudden increase of activity in the Dutch canals and ports. Take Ostend:

    August 28—no barges
    August 31—18 barges
    September 2—70 barges
    September 5—115 barges
    September 6—205 barges

The same pattern had been observed along the coast, at Flushing, Calais, and Dunkirk. And suddenly large numbers of Ju-87s, the Stukas that had been reserved for the invasion, were reappearing on the Pas de Calais airfields. The British codebreakers, with their Enigma machine, were intercepting and reading high-level messages about bomber reinforcement.

On August 30, after the first British raids on Berlin, Hitler met with Goering and withdrew the ban on the bombing of London. He went much further, and told Goering that he wished the Luftwaffe would bomb London in retaliation for the British bombing of Berlin. Within hours Goering had issued a directive to his air fleets, ordering the bombing.

The Luftwaffe was now confident that the end of the Royal Air Force fighter command was just days away. They claimed to have shot down 1,115 aircraft since August 8, and they knew that they had lost 467 planes. Now with the weathermen forecasting a week or ten days of fine weather, they expected to finish the job.

On September 3 Goering met Field Marshal Kesselring and General Sperrle at the Hague. Kesselring said it was a fine idea to bomb London, but Sperrle said he did not think they were ready for that quite yet; the RAF fighters had not been cut down to size.

Kesselring disagreed. His intelligence said that enough had been done and that it was time to switch the offensive. He estimated that the British fighter strength was down to fewer than three hundred Hurricanes and Spitfires. Actually there were seven hundred planes available to the fighter command just then. Kesselring believed that by sending the bombers, escorted heavily by fighters, they could draw the British fighters up to the defense of London and wipe them out.

Fighter Commander Adolf Galland agreed, but he had one caveat. Over London the Me-109s would have only about ten minutes of fighting time before they had to head back for the Channel and fuel on the French side. Sperrle argued, but it was in vain, for the next day Hitler intervened publicly.

Hitler, who had an excellent ear for German public opinion, had recognized the general German concern over the bombings, and decided to do something to counteract it. On September 4, in a speech to social workers at the Berlin Sportpalast, he sensed the two big questions in the German mind: when was the promised invasion of Britain going to come, and what would be done about the night bombings of German cities?

He addressed himself to both questions:

As to the first, he promised his audience that the Germans were going to invade, although he was no more definite than that about the timing.

As to the second question, he said:

"When the British air force drops two or three or four thousand kilograms of bombs, then we will in one night drop 150, 250, 300, or 400,000 kilograms."

The pronouncement was greeted by applause, according to William L. Shirer, the correspondent, who was there.

". . . We will raze their cities to the ground. We will stop the handiwork of these night pirates, so help us God!"

By this time the audience was hysterical with joy.

After the speech, contemplating its effects, Hitler decided that the Luftwaffe would change its focus. Instead of continuing to concentrate on the British air defenses, the German air force would begin the pulverization of Britain's cities, with particular emphasis on London.

On September 5 *Oberkommando* Wehrmacht issued a special Hitler directive, calling on the Luftwaffe to begin "harassing attacks" on the British cities, and especially on London.

Field Marshal Wilhelm Keitel, the chief of staff of OKW, fully agreed. He was concerned about softening Britain up for the invasion, which was still very much on the German schedule, and like many generals, he believed that a huge air assault on London would bring the British government to chaos and make the invasion easy or even unnecessary. The date for the invasion had just been changed from September 15 to September 21 because of the failure so far of the Luftwaffe to knock out the RAF.

On September 5 British bomber command made its first major attack on the invasion ports, and the following day all RAF units were placed on alert:

"Attack probable within the next three days."

General Alan Brooke wrote in his diary that day that all reports indicated the invasion was coming. Ships were collecting, dive-bombers concentrated—all the signs were there.

Then, on the afternoon of September 7, 1940, 625 bombers and 648 fighters took off from the German airfields, heading for Britain's capital city. Riding in an open Merecedes staff car, Reichsmarschal Goering in a long leather coat drove up the road toward Saint Omer with Bruno Loerzer, commander of *Fliegerkorps* 11. He had traveled from his headquarters. Kesselring was also in the car. Goering had come to watch the opening of the "final stage" of the Battle of Britain.

"I have taken personal command of the Luftwaffe in its war against England," he said in a national broadcast.

By 2 o'clock that afternoon, Marshal Goering and Marshal Kesselring and their staffs had moved to a picnic ground at Cap Gris Nez, where the high cliff gave an excellent view of the whole area and England beyond the Channel. Soon they heard the rumble of many aircraft engines. Goering stood up and focused his binoculars on the first spearhead of Heinkel bombers, which was circling ten miles away, waiting to form up with the ME-109 escort high above. Now, said Goering, let the battle begin.

As if warned, a group of American news correspondents drove down to the mouth of the Thames Estuary, through the streets of the working-class district, in sight of the ships, the warehouses, and the paraphernalia of the port of London with the big, ugly round oil tanks in full view, a primary target for any bomber. The newsmen crossed the river and stopped at a place that gave them a view of the river, from Tilbury to the middle of London.

At the radar station at Foreness, on the extremity of Kent country jutting into the Channel, the first motion was observed. A WAAF corporal at Dover reported the news, a big buildup in the air over the Pas de Calais region. At 3:54 P.M., a track plotter at the fighter command headquarters at Bentley Priory placed a plot on the big map table, showing more than twenty aircraft coming in. Within seconds other reports followed, each building the force assembling on the plot table.

Air Marshal Park ordered eleven squadrons of fighters to scramble, and at Kenley, North Weald, Hendon, and Northolt—all fields that had been bombed again and again—the telephones began to ring. The blue of engine exhausts skirled across the airfields as the pilots manned their planes.

East of London the air raid siren, called Weeping Willie, began to sound its mournful wail, and down on the coast the newsmen could see the white puffs of antiaircraft fire against the blue sky of afternoon. The first flight of German bombers came into view, a ragged formation, and not very strong. Already the British Hurricanes and Spitfires had been alerted and were climbing up to meet them. The planes passed over, but soon a much larger formation of bombers came along, and the antiaircraft fire began again.

In the air, the British pilots waited. Flight Lieutenant James MacArthur of Squadron 609 was on patrol at ten thousand feet near Windsor when he saw about two hundred German aircraft surrounded by antiaircraft fire. He led the squadron up and started to attack. Another pilot also watched them come. "It was a breathtaking sight," he said.

Many of the British fighters were in the wrong places. By experience they had learned to expect attack on the airfields, so they were patrolling near their fields. But they saw nothing, and suddenly it became apparent: all these planes were heading for one spot, London.

The Hurricanes of Squadron 501 and Squadron 249 were the first to engage the enemy that day. As usual, they were outnumbered by the Me-109s, by about ten to one. But they rushed in to attack the bombers, and the Me-109s sped down to attack them.

The air battle began. Up in what was obviously London, fires had broken out, and the newsmen could see the billows of smoke, some of them from the oil storage tanks which were sending their oily vapors to the sky encased in red flame. At 5:00 P.M., the first wave of 320 bombers flew up the Thames in ragged little groups and began dropping bombs on Woolwich Arsenal, the gas works, power stations, railroad depots, and the docks.

But now the Me-109s were deserting the fold—low on fuel, they had to head home—and the British fighters were beginning to attack in strength. The formations of bombers had already been made more ragged by antiaircraft fire, and in a few minutes as the bombers headed home, Squadron 303 brought down eleven of them. Soon the waterfront was a mass of flame, and at one neighborhood, Silvertown, the people were engulfed and had to be evacuated by water on the river. It was two hours before the "all clear" sounded. Darkness fell, and shortly after eight o'clock that evening, a second wave of 250 bombers came in.

The fires along the river had turned the sky smoky and the moon red. The Germans were sending their aircraft in by small units, almost like a precision drill, delivering big bombs, which burst with *crump-p-ping* noises, and sent spurts of flame through the night sky. Next day, CBS correspondent Edward R. Murrow found one bomb crater that he said was the largest he had ever seen anywhere in his coverage of many wars.

After that, smaller waves kept coming until four-thirty on the morning of September 8. When the count was made, it was learned that the Germans had lost forty-one aircraft and the British twenty-eight.

That afternoon of September 7, as the bombs rained down on London, the British chiefs of staff met, and as the bombs blasted and blazed the London docks, they decided that the possibility of invasion was imminent and they issued orders to the army to get ready. There was no need to issue special instructions to the navy or the air force, which had been operating at full readiness for weeks. But the army and the Home Guard had to have attention.

So the code word "Cromwell" was sent out from headquarters at 8:00 P.M.

All troops in the London region and coastal England and two corps in reserve were ordered to report to battle stations to prepare to fend off invaders. That night the Home Guard panicked. They had been cautioned to watch for parachute invasion, which was expected in conjunction with the coastal landings. That night parachutists were seen dropping all over the countryside; the signal for parachute attack—the peal of church bells—rang out all across the country, and some perfectly good bridges were blown up. The confusion was considerable in the Kent and Surrey countryside.

Britain's fighter command, the exhausted fighter squadrons, and the airfields had gotten a reprieve, and none too soon. A few days earlier, Prime Minister Churchill had visited Manston Airdrome to discover that although four clear days had passed since the field was last raided, the craters on the runways remained unfilled and the airfield was serviceable only for a handful of planes at a time. About 150 people were trying to fill the craters, largely with wheelbarrows and hand equipment. What was needed, of course, was bulldozers and earth-moving equipment, but it was not in use. That situation at Manston had to be multiplied to include all the airfields that had been so severely under attack for a month, to see the picture of a waning British air capability.

From August 24 the Germans had shifted from attacking the coastal airfields to attacking bases inland. They had done great damage to fighter command's communications system. Twenty-four of the Luftwaffe's thirty-three heaviest attacks had fallen on airfields. The key targets, as it turned out, were the sector stations. After the attack of August 18, Kenley had been able to operate only two of its three squadrons. Only one of the seven master sector stations (Northolt) had escaped attack. At Biggin Hill the damage had been so great as to reduce capability to a single squadron.

Between August 24 and September 6 the RAF had lost 295 Hurricanes and Spitfires, including eighteen in accidents. Another 171 had been badly damaged. The losses had been replaced from reserves, but production was not keeping up, for during that time, only 269 planes had been produced.

But now the focus had changed, and the fighter squadrons and their personnel had time to rest, repair, and regroup.

On September 8 at 7:30 P.M., the German attack on London was renewed. In those first two nights, 842 people died and 2,347 were wounded.

Next day began the speculation about the German invasion, which everyone knew was supposed to come sometime around September 15.

With the respite, Prime Minister Churchill set out in his special train to view the defenses of his nation, particularly in Kent and Sussex. And every night the Germans returned. The bombing soon assumed a pattern: For the first few hours the bombers dropped incendiaries, apparently hoping to start fires that would serve as beacons for the bombers carrying high explosives. The heavy attacks came at around midnight.

Within four days, Correspondent Murrow reported, Londoners had become old hands at the bombing. Every night they could be seen queuing up in front of the big public air raid shelters, waiting for the shelters to open their doors when the air raid sirens began. They brought mattresses and blankets and food and drink to sustain them through the night.

Air Chief Marshal Dowding, with considerable relief, began moving his fighter squadrons around, sending to rest those that had been worn to a frazzle in recent nights. Squadron No. 43 had just lost its commander and a flight commander.

It was badly understrength in pilots and planes. It was sent north. Squadron 111 was down to seven Hurricanes, most of which were unfit to fly. As soon as the aircraft could be moved, the Squadron headed north.

The first military reports of the bombing of London indicated to the British that the Luftwaffe plan showed careful study. The bombing was very effective against railway lines and stations, and the airmen did not think that this was accidental.

The effect of the bombing on London's East End was dreadful. Most of this area was slum, ancient houses barely standing the ravages of time, and the bombing had caused street after street of buildings to collapse, with scarcely a house standing in some blocks. In this area about 450 people were blown up or killed in the wreckage, and more than twice as many injured.

After that first night in the East End, there was a daily exodus that began about one-thirty in the afternoon. The poor of London thought, suspected, or said they knew, that the "toffs" in the West End had better protection than they, so thousands of them headed west for the safety of the shelters there. The people assembled their blankets, sandwiches, the belongings they would need for the night. At about two they would set off, perhaps for the basement of Dickens and Jones's department store in Oxford Street, or for Edgware, Golders Green, Tottenham Court Road—traveling on the underground trains. Oxford Street was as crowded as on a sale day. Dickens and Jones's shelter did not open until 7:00 P.M., and then only the first seven hundred people were let in, so it was important to be early. The people marched down two flights of stairs and into the big, clean basement. Soon the concrete floor was covered with bodies stretched out on blankets. Some had brought pillows and cushions, some had beach chairs. The store staff served refreshments, and queues formed to receive them. Street musicians came in to play, and pass the hat for the Spitfire Fund.

By ten-thirty at night, almost everyone was either asleep or somnolent, and the snoring could be heard two floors above. At five-thirty an air raid warden with a megaphone would appear at the door and shout, "All clear, all clear," and the room would rise up, the blankets would be rolled, the pillows stuffed somewhere, the empty sandwich bags jammed into trash receptacles, and the trek back to the East End would begin, to be reversed again in early afternoon.

Every night the bombers came, and soon the East End began to become barren. On the doors of the standing houses were notes left for relatives and friends: "Gone to Dagenham . . ." "Find me in Chadwell Heath . . ." The people were moving out from the center of the metropolis, out but still staying in London. In one street only a fifth of the residents remained, and they evacuated every night but returned in the morning to tidy up and prepare for the next night's ordeal.

Reichsmarschal Goering was elated with the reported results of his first London raid in spite of the losses, and buoyed up by the reports of succeeding raids in the following week. But the German naval general staff took a much more pragmatic view of events.

"There is no sign of the defeat of the enemy's air force over southern England and in the Channel area," said the German navy war diary on September 10, four days after the daily bombing of London began. "And this is vital to a further judgment of the situation."

The invasion was still scheduled for September 21, but Hitler had said he would give three days notice before the signal to go. The navy did not believe the signs indicated that the invasion would succeed, under the current circumstances.

"The preliminary attacks by the Luftwaffe have indeed achieved a noticeable weakening of the enemy's fighter defense, so that considerable German fighter superiority can be assumed over the English area. However, we have not yet attained the operational conditions which the naval staff stipulated to the Supreme Command as being essential for the enterprise, namely, undisputed air supremacy in the Channel area and the elimination of the enemy's air activity in the assembly area of the German naval forces and ancillary shipping."

It was all very well and good propaganda for the Luftwaffe to lambast London, said the navy, but "it would be in conformity with the timetable preparations for 'Sea Lion' if the Luftwaffe would now concentrate less on London and more on Portsmouth and Dover, as well as on the naval ports in and near the operational area.''

But by the time this note was written, the navy did not dare come out to demand the change in bombing, because Hitler had been persuaded by Goering that it would not be long now, that London would be destroyed, and that then the invasion probably would not be necessary, and if it was necessary, it would be a walk-in.

When Admiral Raeder contemplated the coming days, and the date of September 21 for the invasion, he saw what a disaster was building for his naval forces. Finally on September 12 he summoned the courage to beard Hitler with the cold facts.

The air war is being conducted as an ''absolute air war'' without regard to the present requirements of the naval war, and outside the framework of preparation for ''Sea Lion.'' In its present form the air war cannot assist preparations for Sea Lion which are predominantly in the hands of the navy. In particular one cannot discern any effort on the part of the Luftwaffe to engage the units of the British fleet which are now able to operate almost unmolested in the Channel, and this will prove extremely dangerous to the transportation. Thus the main safeguard against British naval forces would have to be the minefields, which, as repeatedly explained to the Supreme Command, cannot be regarded as reliable protection for shipping.

The fact remains that up to now the intensified air war has not contributed towards the landing operation, hence for operational and military reasons the execution of the landing cannot yet be considered.

There it was: the stark fact that the invasion of Britain was far too risky to undertake at the moment. So the pressure was then put squarely on the Luftwaffe, either to bring Britain to its knees through the air attack on the cities, as Goering boasted he could do, or to turn to the demolition of the Royal Navy. Goering insisted on continuing his course. The destruction of London, he said, was imminent, and it would end the war.

# CHAPTER 11

# *London Can Take It*

On September 7, after sending the bombers off to London, Reichsmarschal Hermann Goering waited impatiently at Cap Gris Nez for their return. His wife, Emmy, telephoned him there, and he boasted to her: "I've sent my bombers to London; London's in flames."

A radio reporter was on the air, telling of the battle. Goering seized the microphone.

"This is a historic moment. After all the attacks on Berlin these last nights, the führer decided to order a monster reprisal against the British Empire.

"I personally have taken command of the attack and have heard the roar of victorious German squadrons, which for the first time have struck the enemy right to the heart."

This exchange shows the major reason for Goering's survival and prosperity in the Third Reich. For the fact was that he had opposed the bombing of London, and Hitler had forced the issue over Goering's vigorous objections. Goering had erred in calling off the assault on the British radar stations, but even so, by September 7, victory over the RAF was within the Luftwaffe's grasp. The two-week offensive against the British airfields had cost the British a daily average of 21 fighters, with over 7 pilots killed each day, for a total of 295 fighters downed and 103 pilots killed, and 170 aircraft badly damaged and 128 pilots wounded. Here is the assessment of

Peter Townsend, one of Britain's leading pilots.

"During those two desperate bloody weeks of the airfield offensive the Luftwaffe was never nearer to defeating Fighter Command, even though Dowding's squadrons themselves were making unprecedented slaughter among the Luftwaffe: 378 aircraft, 27 daily. But British fighter and pilot losses were not the whole story; the appalling damage to ops rooms and communications nearly paralyzed the control system."

That control system was the secret of Britain's successful defense, with about 10 percent of the number of planes employed as the enemy, but it was becoming unraveled, with several control centers in ruins and the communications of others being held together with temporary patching of daily damage.

Air Vice Marshal Keith Rodney Park, the director of Fighter Group 11, which covered southeastern England, the area bearing the brunt of the attack, sensed that something was changing. That afternoon of September 7, as he flew above the maelstrom that was the London docks in flame, Park noted with somewhat rueful satisfaction that the change in the German strategy, assaulting civilian London, was going to save the RAF.

German General Theo Osterkamp later said, "It was with tears of rage and dismay that on the very point of victory, I saw the decisive battle against the British fighters stopped for the benefit of attacking London."

The decision was Hitler's, first made on that fateful August 30 in the meeting with Goering, but amplified and confirmed in Hitler's Sportspalast speech to the social workers, and then annealed into policy. Goering went along with very good grace and embraced this new policy, but later he said it had been wrong, that the Luftwaffe should have continued the fight against the airfields.

I believe the plan would have been successful, but as a result of the führer's speech about retribution, in which he asked that London be attacked immediately, I had to follow the other course. I wanted to attack the airfields first, thus creating a prerequisite for attacking London. I spoke to the führer about my plans in order to try to have him agree I should attack the first ring of RAF fields around London, but he insisted he wanted to have London attacked for political reasons and for retribution.

I considered the attacks on London useless and I told the führer again and again that inasmuch as I knew the English people as well as I did my own people, I could never force them to their knees by attacking London. We might be able to subdue the Dutch people by such measures, but not the British.

That night of September 7, Goering went back to his special train called Asia, and then to his headquarters in Paris. Whatever his forebodings, he proceeded to implement the führer's plan of terrorizing London. He divided London into two sectors, east and west. The dock area of the east was first to be bombed, but then he would turn his attention to the west.

Fighter ace Adolf Galland came in for a meeting, and Goering asked him what he needed to make the Luftwaffe fighters more effective. "Give me a squadron of Spitfires," Galland said. Goering's mouth opened and then closed, and he went off in a blazing fury, mumbling to himself.

On September 8 the *Volkischer Beobachter*, the Nazi party newspaper, trumpeted the word of the new campaign against England.

"Last night the enemy again attacked the Reich capital. Therefore the Luftwaffe has started to attack the city of London with strong forces."

That first day's attack was the most successful of the war from the Luftwaffe point of view. First factor was the element of surprise. Until this date the Germans had been forbidden to bomb London. One pilot who flew over the city in a Ju-88 noted how clear the night air was that night. "Everywhere the German bombers were swarming. Everything was lit up by fires like a huge torch in the night. But now for the first time we were allowed to bomb regardless . . ."

The first fighter attacks were scattered, because the British fighters were in the wrong places. The Dorniers and the Heinkels and the Ju-88s bombed at leisure. One pilot took pictures of the burning docks with his own Leica camera, fitted with a telephoto lens. The first wave was very successful, and only thirteen bombers of the first armada failed to return. When the survivors got back to French soil they broadcast the good news of their successful mission.

The first night raid came up from the south, Heinkels with their throbbing engines, crossing Beachy Head at 8:22 P.M., at fifteen thousand feet. They were unescorted, but only two Hurricanes came out to meet them. Later a Blenheim and a Beaufighter came up, but the attacks were uncoordinated and not very successful. The bombing was very easy for the German aircrews that first day. Most of the antiaircraft guns were unable to bear on the bombers.

On the morning of September 8, the British faced some important decisions. Was this really a change in direction? Or would the Germans be back working over the airfields again today? Air Marshal Dowding puzzled over the problem. Reconnaissance planes flew over the Channel, but could ascertain no sign of the invasion fleet that was half-expected. In fact, all seemed too quiet for reality. The air marshal was not inclined to look a gift horse too closely in the mouth, and so he did what came naturally. He relieved two of his most battered fighter squadrons from the southern area, No. 43, whose commander, Caesar Hull, had been shot down and killed the previous day, and John Thompson's Squadron 111 with its seven remaining Hurricanes.

Nothing much happened that day, but as night fell, the tenor of activity moved. The air raid sirens began to sound, and as night darkened, the German bombers came. On this second night, over four hundred Londoners were killed.

Perhaps two hundred bombers attacked. On this night the antiaircraft fire was more effective. During the day many guns had been moved to spots where they could fire over central London.

On September 9 the bombers came up the Thames Estuary again, although some went to Southampton. By this time Air Group 11 and Air Group 12 had gotten organized and they went up to meet the estimated two hundred bombers, breaking up the formations and causing them to jettison bomb loads, which then fell all over London and in the suburbs. Buckingham Palace grounds received a few jettisoned bombs, although no one was hurt. That night Somerset House, Victoria station, and parts of Holborn were bombed.

On September 10 the bombers were back, but not in much force, more attention being devoted to the Liverpool area. The weather was drizzly; that may have been part of the reason.

On September 11 air intelligence officers were puzzling over the significance of the London bombings, and reading meanings into the evidence that might have been coincidences. They marveled at the heavy damage done to communications, many railroad stations struck and lines torn up. Did this have implications for the invasion? There were still no visible signs of the armada they expected to sail out from the far shore of the Channel. That day three attacks on London came in the daylight hours, and one of them included the bombing of Buckingham Palace again. The royal family was in residence, and the king wrote about the event in his diary:

"All of a sudden we heard an aircraft making a zooming noise above us, saw two bombs falling past the opposite side of the Palace and then heard two resounding crashes as the bombs fell in the quadrangle about thirty yards away. We looked at each other and then we were out into the passage as fast as we could get there. The whole thing happened in a matter of seconds. We all wondered why we weren't dead. Six bombs had been dropped. The aircraft was seen coming straight down the Mall below the clouds, having dived through the clouds. There is no doubt it was a direct attack on Buckingham Palace."

No doubt at all, given free rein as they had been, some of the young bucks of the Luftwaffe decided that the destruction of Buckingham Palace would be an excellent idea, and several squadrons competed for the honor. It was, however a very bad idea. What it did was raise British morale, not lower it. Propaganda Minister Goebbels first ordered that the stories about the bombing of the palace be used and amplified. "Enke gives a brilliantly incisive report on the bombing of London, which will provide superb material for propaganda at home and abroad. I order it to be used accordingly."

But a few days later, Goebbels had a slightly different view. "We bomb London and other cities with the usual quantity of high explosives despite the fog. In London meanwhile the illusion-mongering campaign is being continued and showing some success, especially in the U.S.A. where they are willing to accept it at face value. I receive a report from the U.S.A. which outlines the unpleasant results of this propaganda. I will now take strong countermeasures. The press and the radio will be drawn firmly into the service of anti-English propaganda.''

The fact was that the British people took the bombing of the palace quite calmly. They seemed to feel that it was fine that the king and queen were sharing the general hardship.

CBS correspondent Edward R. Murrow, who was doing the most evocative reporting of the London war, said that Londoners were not particularly aroused by the bombing, they seemed to expect that the royal family would share the difficulties. In fact, Murrow indicated, the bombing of Buckingham Palace seemed to bother the Americans more than it did the British.

The British people were doing very poorly during this first week of the bombing. Correspondent Murrow went out to buy a hat, and found his favorite hattery had been blown to bits. He went to see about some shoes and found that the windows of his shoe store had been blown out. He went for a haircut; the windows of the barbershop were gone, but the barber was there calmly cutting hair. He went to a shop to buy some flashlight batteries, and bought three. The clerk said he needn't buy so many because they had a whole winter's supply on hand. But what if they got bombed out? said Murrow.

''Of course we'll be here,'' said the shopman placidly. ''We've been in business here for a hundred and fifty years.''

September 11 was a bad day for the British defenders. They shot down twenty-five German planes, but they lost twenty-nine of their own. That kind of odds could be disastrous if the process continued.

September 12, however, was a more Londony kind of a day, with drizzle. The rain did not help the Germans, and many missions were aborted. Only four German planes were shot down, and the British did not lose a single aircraft.

Tom Harrisson, in his book *Living Through the Blitz*, gave

an account of the emotional changes that the bombing brought. On September 9 he began to follow the adventures of seven newly recruited waitresses of a Lyons restaurant, the Corner House at Marble Arch, one of the largest restaurants in London. The "Nippy trainees," they were called. On the morning of September 9 the women were assembled at a new women's table and were babbling away about the bombing they had seen in the past two days. They spoke of the intensity in the East End—not a single street in Bow that hadn't got a bomb.

They spoke of serving the customers—one had done so and reported on a maggot in the salad.

They spoke of Lord Haw Haw, the British traitor propagandist for Goebbels in Berlin, who had said that the Germans would bomb all the Lyons Corner Houses because they were Jewish, and everyone laughed.

They spoke of "screaming bombs" and the customers they would be serving and their impressions of the bombing. They were all gay and chattery.

After the women had finished eating their dinners, the supervisor told them that this afternoon they were going to go to school at the Strand Corner House in Trafalgar Square, so they trouped out to the bus stop and they joked with the bus driver as they made their way to Trafalgar. When they arrived, the crowd was augmented until there were sixteen women and nine men attending the class. The instructor was a woman about forty years old who first talked about the job, and then about Lyons Restaurants, and their places as cogs in a great machine.

The class continued, and as evening drew near, the women began to get a little edgy, starting at small noises. Then the siren sounded and the women began to be very nervous. The instructor tried to calm them; there was no need to go down to the shelter until the "danger overhead" signal sounded. Since the firm had a watcher on the roof, everything was perfectly safe for the moment.

The lesson went on. Changing the tablecloth. "Now, girls . . ."

Then the danger alert sounded, three sharp blasts.

The enemy was overhead; it was time to go to the shelter.

The men showed bravado as they moved to the shelter; the women held hands for comfort. The shelter was deep in the basement of the building, alongside the boiler room; benches stood against the walls.

Soon the shelter was full of people. Except for talking in low tones, it was very quiet. The instructor came back, and said that it was all right to go up again and resume the lesson. They listened for a half hour and then everyone went to the messroom for tea. They were having tea when the sound of gunfire interrupted. The blinds were drawn, and then a warden came in to order the messroom cleared away.

Once again the group went to the basement. There the women became quite cheerful and spoke with feeling of what they would do with Hitler if they could get hold of him. "Cook 'im h'in a pie," said one.

After fifteen minutes the raid ended and they went back to duty.

That was Monday, the second day of the bombing. Each afternoon after that, they were in class when the air raid siren sounded and the procedure was repeated.

For the first week, all went well. Latecomers were not scolded, and the supervisors were very sympathetic about personal problems. The uniform supervisor told them about the rules they could wink at (your collar does *not* have to be sewn to the dress). The floor manager told them he was winking at five minutes or so of tardiness.

By the time of the fourth alert on Wednesday (September 11), the women had become so used to the processes that the air of nervousness had quite vanished. But by Friday the novelty had worn off and the women of Marble Arch decided they would not go to Trafalgar Square, because they were sure to get an air raid and be stuck there all night. Only eight of the twenty-five students made the scene. The others went home.

By the second week, the truancy factor had become very large, and the Lyons officials were growing impatient. The new women were coming in later and later, sometimes three hours late. And they did not care. There seemed to be a sort of competition as to who could be latest and get away with it. The supervisors who had seemed so sympathetic now appeared as ogres. By the end of the second week, morale at Lyons had gone from bad to worse, and the celebrated efficiency was a thing of the past. London and Londoners were settling in for a long, long haul.

The Blitz bombing of London had changed the lives of everyone, adding a whole new element to the lives of the people. One got up in the morning to go to work, then in the afternoon work life was disrupted by the bombing and one went into the air raid life. Then in the evening, perhaps, or later at night, people tried to pick up their personal lives.

Social life came to a standstill for a time, until people began to adjust to the routine and to make it work for them. Tom Harrisson's six Nippy girls by the end of a month had managed to resume some sort of life, with boyfriends, cinemas, pubs, and West End outings, in spite of the bombs.

And the war went on.

What now of the invasion? On September 3 the Germans had moved it back to September 21, with a firm decision to be made ten days in advance (in deference to the navy).

On September 11 Prime Minister Churchill told the British, "This effort of the Germans to secure daylight mastery of the air over England is, of course, the crux of the whole war." He also said he did not think the invasion decision could be long delayed. "We must regard this week as a very important period in our history. It ranks with the days when the Spanish Armada was approaching or when Nelson stood between us and Napoleon's Grand Army at Boulogne."

On September 11 Hitler delayed a decision for another three days days, which meant the invasion could not come before the twenty-fourth, and on the fourteenth he had postponed the decision for another three days, which moved the date up to September 27. By this time, everybody knew, the weather would be worsening rapidly and time was running out.

*Oberkommando* Luftwaffe gave out the most optimistic reports. They were full of error, but both sides were exaggerating their successes and minimizing their failures. But on the eleventh a hundred bombers did get through to London and hit the supermarine engine factory at Southampton, and the RAF was outfought that day by the Luftwaffe.

At German naval headquarters the tension was enormous, and Admiral Raeder complained that the RAF and the Royal Navy had made the major invasion ports of Ostend, Dunkirk, Calais, and Boulogne unsafe as night anchorages.

The Germans had noted that the weather was worsening on September 12 and September 13 and the defenses had a respite from large-scale attacks, but the Germans continued to send single aircraft aloft to make attacks.

On September 13 Hitler called Reichsmarschal Goering to an emergency meeting in the chancellery in Berlin. Hitler was in a predicament. Herr Goebbels had put him on the spot with a public prediction of the invasion, which now kept being updated, but it was all accompanied by loud music and shouts: "*Wir fliegen gegen England.*" True, but when would the invasion really begin? Everyone in Berlin was waiting for the welcome news.

Goering was all confidence. The führer could leave everything to him, he said. The RAF had only about fifty Spitfires left, he said. The bombing of London had produced disaster, he said. The weather, as usual, had caused problems, but in four or five more days the Luftwaffe would produce the total victory.

So Hitler's sagging spirit was revived with promises, and at lunch Hitler expressed great optimism to the crowd of some twenty. Operation Sea Lion was no longer going to be necessary, he said. Goering was going to do the job all alone.

On September 14 Field Marshal Kesselring sent over Ju-88s and Heinkels, which bombed the southern suburbs of London, and Eastbourne and Brighton.

That day Hitler met Admiral Raeder at 3:00 P.M. General Brauchitsch was there representing the army, and General Jeschonnek representing the Luftwaffe. Goering had hurried back to the Pas de Calais to supervise the final rites for England. Just before the meeting, the admiral gave Hitler a memo:

"The present air situation does not allow the undertaking of Operation Sea Lion," it said. "Meanwhile, it is indispensable that Sea Lion not be abandoned."

This attitude presented a new problem for Hitler. Here was

the invasion again, and Raeder said it was going to be absolutely necessary.

So everyone was still on pins and needles. That day General Busch, head of the Sixteenth Army, which would do most of the fighting, signed the order for execution of Operation Sea Lion. It was also signed by Admiral Luetjens, fleet commander at Boulogne, who would play a major tactical role.

A new order would follow on September 17, Hitler assured everyone. Meanwhile give Goering his extra few days to finish the job. He had promised a really important effort for the morrow, September 15.

The assessment was that the Luftwaffe had nearly accomplished what it needed to do, but not quite. The proof was in the heavy attacks on the Channel ports, where the invasion fleet was mustering. As long as the British could continue to do that, and as long as the fighters came up to meet the attacking bombers, then it was too dangerous to mount the invasion. It was now almost an hour-to-hour show, with the Germans trying to deliver a knockout blow. On their success or failure in this regard in the next few hours would rest the fate of the invasion.

# CHAPTER 12

# The Great Air Battle

Early on the morning of September 15, 1940, with an uncanny sense of history, Prime Minister Churchill knew that this day would be vital in the Battle of Britain, and so his car was called to the prime minister's country house at Chequers, and he and Mrs. Churchill drove to the headquarters of No. 11 Fighter Group at Uxbridge. After five days of intermittent rain, the day had dawned fine and clear, just the sort of weather that the Luftwaffe wanted for a major daylight raid. They arrived at ten-thirty that morning.

Although overall command of the fighters was exercised from the fighter headquarters at Stanmore, the actual dispatch and direction of the fighting was handled at Uxbridge, which controlled the south of England, through underground fighter stations located in each of the six countries. No. 11 Group consisted of twenty-five squadrons of Spitfires and Hurricanes under Air Vice Marshal Keith Rodney Park.

At Uxbridge the Churchills were taken down into the bomb-proof operations room fifty feet underground. The room was really a small theater, about sixty feet wide, extending two stories. The Churchills sat in the "dress circle," above the large map table, and around it stood twenty young men and women, each accompanied by a telephone assistant. Opposite the Churchills, the entire wall was covered by a large blackboard, divided into six columns, which represented the six fighter stations. Each column was further divided into spaces, each representing one fighter squadron, divided by lateral lines, and festooned with light bulbs. The lowest row of light bulbs when lit showed the squadrons that were standing by, ready at two minutes notice to scramble. The second row from the bottom showed the squadrons "at readiness," which meant they could be in the air in five minutes. The third row showed the squadrons "available," which meant they could operate in twenty minutes. The fourth row up from the bottom showed the squadrons that were actually in the air. The fifth row showed the squadrons that had sighted the enemy. The sixth row up showed with red lights those squadrons that were engaging the enemy, and the top row showed the squadrons that were returning to base.

On the left side of the amphitheater sat five officers in a glass box. It was their duty to evaluate the information coming in to this nerve center from the fifty thousand men and women of the Observer Corps. First the radar warned of objects in the air approaching the coast, and then the observers, with field glasses and portable telephones, refined the information as the objects became aircraft heading inland. This information was first sorted out by several rooms full of people, and the results were telephoned to the officer supervising that area, sitting in his glass box. He directed the young men and women in his sector of the big table, who showed with small discs the enemy approaching.

On the right-hand side of the blackboard stood another glass box, occupied by army officers, who reported on the activity of the two hundred antiaircraft batteries. One of their principal tasks was to prevent the antiaircraft guns from firing on the British fighters as they closed with the Germans. This system had been refined over the years and now presented a picture of controlled efficiency.

When the Churchills arrived, all was quiet. Everyone was waiting, knowing already that the enemy was coming. Although anyone could predict from the barometer and a look at the sky that it would be fine weather, the Luftwaffe as usual sent its Heinkel reconnaissance planes out before dawn. One of these was discovered by two pilots of Squadron No. 87, who shot the plane down over the sea before breakfast.

By 7:00 A.M., the attack was shaping up on the airfields as Field Marshal Kesselring prepared to make the great effort to deliver final victory to Reichsmarschal Goering. Morale was suffering on the German side from too many contradicting orders, too much speculation, too long a delay in ordering Operation Sea Lion, and too much vituperation from Goering, who was blaming his subordinates for all that had gone wrong with the Eagle campaign.

The Churchills settled in their seats. At about a quarter to eleven, the word reached Uxbridge that an attack was forming over the Pas de Calais. Fifteen minutes later, the raid plotters began moving their plots on the boards.

At eleven-thirty the first enemy planes crossed the coast of Kent. The first showed forty-plus Luftwaffe planes coming from the Dieppe area. The bulbs along the bottom row of the panel began to light up as the squadrons came to "stand by." Then the plots grew more numerous on the table, twenty-plus, forty-plus, sixty-plus, and even eighty-plus—and half an hour after the Churchills had arrived, the board and the lights were moving rapidly. A major air battle was shaping up.

The controller at No. 11 Air Group had plenty of time to put up ten squadrons and order them to form into wings before the first Germans crossed the coastline. The Duxford wing was formed up at 11:25, and the enemy did not cross over until 11:35.

The plotters moved their discs along the lines of approach of the enemy. The blackboard lights showed the fighter squadrons getting ready, getting into the air, and moving toward the enemy, until soon there were only five squadrons left "at readiness."

The first series of air encounters, strung out over southern England, began then. A squadron could stay aloft for seventy or eighty minutes, but then had to land to refuel. If the planes engaged the enemy, after five minutes all ammunition was exhausted and they must land to rearm. This was the vulnerable period, in which the enemy might arrive in fresh numbers, and destroy aircraft on the ground. The job of fighter command was to see that there were always planes in the air to engage the enemy and prevent the bombing and strafing of the airfields then.

Near the end of the hour the board showed that most squadrons were engaged. Sitting next to Prime Minister Churchill and Air Vice Marshal Park was a young officer whose job it was to interpret the instructions of the air marshal to the fighter stations. On his orders the individual fighter squadrons moved. Soon the air marshal was walking up and down behind, watching every move of the board and the lights, and issuing an occasional order to supplement those of his subordinate.

All the squadrons were in the air, many of them fighting, and some were returning for fuel and ammunition. The lower line of bulbs was dark; Britain at that moment did not have a squadron in reserve in the fighting sector. Air Vice Marshal Park then telephoned Air Chief Marshal Dowding at Stanmore, asking for three squadrons from No. 12 Group to be ready in case of another major attack while the squadrons of No. 11 Group were regassing and rearming, and this was done. London was again covered. The tension in the room was continuous, but the tenor was low, and around the plotting table all that could be heard was a "subdued hum" of the low voices of the plotters and their telephone assistants. The young officer next to Churchill gave orders in a calm, low voice. The effect was that of some great human machine directing the movement in the air.

The prime minister did not then know it, but the battle had reached a crucial stage.

Group 11's Operations Room put up twelve squadrons, and they fought the enemy all the way into London. One five-squadron wing caught up with the Germans on the southern edge of the metropolis. The British fighters broke up the formations, and the bombs were scattered for miles across the southern districts. A bomb hit Buckingham Palace again, and another fell on the grounds. A Dornier exploded and crashed through the roof of Victoria station. Those three squadrons from No. 12 Group were called into action.

"What other reserves have you?" Churchill asked.

"There are none," said the air marshal impassively.

The prime minister looked very worried, as if he realized that the crisis had come. In another five minutes the squadrons were descending to refuel and rearm, and the situation appeared to be desperate. But the Germans had the same problem, and as the first British squadrons began to land, it was apparent that the Germans were turning and heading back to France.

The Churchills left the underground amphitheater then and the prime minister went home to Chequers to take his afternoon nap. Meanwhile the air battle was resumed.

Reichsmarschal Goering's train was sitting on a siding at Boulogne that day, and the commander of the Luftwaffe was waiting impatiently for news of the battle. "They must be reaching the limit of their resources," said his aide. "Today's assault should complete the operation."

In the air above London, one of the bomber pilots, watching as a great batch of the 370 British fighters that took to the air approached his formation, recalled Georing's last remarks: "Look out," he shouted, "here come those last fifty Spitfires!" And then his words trailed off in the chatter of machine guns and the booming of aerial cannon.

The Me-109 pilots, doing their best to protect the bombers, saw the red lights of their fuel gauges begin to glow and knew it was time to turn around. Forty of the Me-109s did not make it to their fields, but crash-landed on the beaches and in fields along the French shore.

At Cap Blanc Nez Field Marshal Kesselring got the reports of the damage done to his squadrons, and called Goering in his special train.

"We cannot keep up this rate," he said in anguish. "We are falling below the standard of safety."

The Germans came back in even greater numbers. Group 11 scrambled twenty-three squadrons, getting three squadrons from Group 10. Three waves of German bombers, Dorniers and Heinkels, came up the coast, apparently got confused, and milled around for a time, giving the British defenders a chance to get into the air, and also wasting the fuel supplies of the Me-109s. Over the southern suburbs the British fighters met the enemy, and the Me-109s defended valiantly, keeping their charges away from the enemy fighters. But all too soon for the Germans the Me-109s had to leave the scene again, and now the British Spitfires and Hurricanes were among the bombers. Most of the bombs were again jettisoned over the suburbs. There were a few other raids than the ones on London that day. One formation raided Portland, and another hit the Woolston Supermarine works at Southampton. The raid came just before six o'clock in the evening, and there was not a British fighter in sight, but the antiaircraft gunners put up such a barrage that the Germans did not score a single bomb hit on the vital factory.

Prime Minister Churchill slept through the whole afternoon's raids, and it was past 8:00 P.M. when he awakened. By that time the battle was over, and the results were being assessed. Churchill's private secretary brought him bad news and good news. The bad news was that losses at sea to submarines were worse than ever. The good news was: "We have shot down one hundred and eighty Germans, for a loss of forty."

It was not true. The next morning the London *Daily Telegraph* and other newspapers trumpeted the news of the great victory, claiming that 175 German planes had been destroyed. That was not true either. But it was true that sixty Luftwaffe planes had been downed, with a loss of twenty-six British fighter planes. It was indeed a great victory for the British. And that night the British bombers visited the invasion ports from Le Havre to Antwerp, and bombed the shipping targets again. The navy called for more antiaircraft guns for the area.

On September 16 the Luftwaffe mounted a few attacks, mostly against London, losing nine aircraft while the British lost but a single fighter. That day Hermann Goering called his chief executives of the Luftwaffe to his headquarters train at Boulogne and bellowed at them that the fighters had let the air force down. The fighter commanders tried to argue, but Goering was not listening. What they wanted was to be freed of the necessity to escort the bombers, but Goering held firmly that the bombers were the necessary bait to bring the RAF up into the air to be shot down.

Long forgotten was the original premise of knocking out the RAF communications system. Once again, Goering told his men that a few more days and they would have the British by the throat. Others might look at the statistics: since September 7 the Germans had lost 190 planes against the RAF's loss of 120. But Goering would not listen to that sort of talk.

The next day, September 17, was the all-important day, for the weather and tides experts told the navy, who told Hitler, that if the invasion was not launched by September 27, then it would have to wait until spring. The RAF was out, bombing the invasion ports and sinking barges. The Luftwaffe raided London again, mostly in fighter sweeps. The Germans lost eight planes to the RAF's five. But most important, *Oberkommando* Wehrmacht issued a laconic statement—five words—*Wird Bis Auf Weiteres Verschoben*—"Postponed until further notice." The British would worry about the threat for another few weeks, but it had ended. Goering did not admit it, but the navy could tell him that he had failed, and that the Luftwaffe had lost the battle of the airfields. On September 17 Goering was summoned to Berchtesgaden by Hitler to explain what was going on in the air. As always, he made a blustering case for himself. It was too bad that the weather had slowed operations to the extent that the invasion date for the fall had been lost, he said, but he would finish the job with the Luftwaffe and perhaps no invasion at all would be necessary. He just needed a little more time.

Since there was no alternative, Hitler agreed that the job might be done, and Goering went back to the French coast.

That day, September 17, Prime Minister Churchill also reported to Parliament on the air battle of September 15, which he termed "the most beautiful and fruitful" of any battles fought by the RAF. But the battle was continuing, he said, and would continue. And it did continue; the Luftwaffe bombers raided London and other cities, and nineteen German planes were shot down, while the British lost 12 fighters. That night the German navy began dispersing the ships and boats that had assembled along the far shore of the English Channel. A thousand barges and three thousand other vessels began to move to places where they could become useful again.

Goering, having returned to France and conferred with his Luftwaffe generals, relinquished personal command of the Luftwaffe and traveled to East Prussia, where he had a hunting lodge and preserve. While Goering hunted and brought some of his favorites to hunt with him, including Adolf Galland, the air war continued.

September 19: Rain all day, but at night the Germans raided London.

September 20: Showers during the day, but heavy fighter sweeps were sent toward London and were met by the RAF, with seven Germans and seven RAF planes shot down.

September 21: Clouds and rain. Fighter sweeps in East Kent, no losses on either side.

September 22: London again, but a half-hearted raid.

September 23: A bad day for the British. On a fine night eleven fighters were lost to shoot down nine Luftwaffe planes.

September 24: London and the Spitfire factory at Southampton, particularly. Eleven German planes shot down, four British fighters.

September 25: Attacks on aircraft factories at Plymouth, Portland, and Bristol. Score—13 Luftwaffe losses, four British fighters down.

September 26: A fine day and a fine night. The Germans finally ''got'' the Spitfire factory at Southampton, and gutted it by fire. But by this time the production of the factory had been dispersed because the Ministry of Aircraft Production had seen the handwriting on the wall. So while the loss was serious (thirty people killed), it was not devastating.

September 27 dawned bright and fine. No one in Britain knew that this would be the day for another of the big raids. The German fighters were in the air by eight o'clock in the morning and headed once again for London, with a group of Me-110s and two more bomber waves coming along behind. The British fighters were also up, and they were shooting down planes right and left. Goering was still staying at his hunting lodge, and it was here that he had the news: The Luftwaffe had suffered an enormous defeat in the day's fighting, and thirty-four of the fifty-five planes shot down were German fighters. The British had lost only eight fighters.

Goering was totally depressed, and for the first time he seemed to realize that the Luftwaffe was not winning the Battle of Britain.

# CHAPTER 13

# The War Winds Down

A touch of the comic had relieved the British tension in the third week of September. Anthony Eden, the foreign minister of Britain, was spending a few days at his country house near Dover. He had a telephone call from Prime Minister Churchill on September 22, in which Churchill said that he in turn had just received a telephone call from President Roosevelt warning him that without fail, on absolute authority, the Germans were going to invade the next day.

Eden took a walk down to the white chalk cliffs of Dover and looked over the edge. Below, the water was choppy and the seas were building up, hardly the sort of weather one would choose to land small boats on an enemy shore.

It was all very mysterious, and continued so until the following day, when Roosevelt again telephoned Churchill. It had been a ridiculous mistake, the American president said. Washington had received the information from its code room, where the Japanese naval code had been broken to a certain extent. The message had referred to the invasion of Indochina, which had indeed happened, but someone had misread the symbols to mean Britain, and so the flap had begun.

There was no comic relief for Reichsmarschal Goering. He had still been relaxing at his hunting lodge in East Prussia, entertaining visitors and behaving in his most confident and jolly manner, when he had learned of the disastrous results of the air battle of September 27, 1940.

Goering had been visibly shaken because he had expected so much from the Luftwaffe, and the pilots had been unable to deliver the victory he expected. The Luftwaffe had suffered a stunning defeat—fifty-five planes shot down in the day's raiding, thirty-four of them fighters. The bombing raids had been broken up before they could reach their objectives.

Goering really could not understand why this had occurred. A week earlier he had the most encouraging reports. Erpro 210, the Me-110 precision bombing unit, had sent in a report of a glide bombing attack on the Spitfire works at Woolston on September 24, a raid that had been very successful, knocking out a large part of the plant, and on September 25 serious damage had been done at the Bristol airplane factory at Filton. The British radar and operations rooms had been fooled that day. The Middle Wallop controller had noticed a large buildup of aircraft heading for Western Britain, which seemed to indicate another raid on the Yeovil aircraft factory, and the fighters had been sent that way. But instead, the German planes had made a sharp turn and sixty bombers had descended on the Bristol works, unchallenged except by anti-aircraft force. The bombers let fly from high altitude without serious interference, and their aim was good. Much destruction was caused at the plant; 82 people were killed and 170 were wounded. The success had been very nearly duplicated the following day, September 26, in a repeat raid on that factory, using the same tactics. Once more the British air controller had been fooled and the raiders had come in without opposition. To the Luftwaffe this all added up to their conclusion that the British fighter force was failing, when the actuality was that misjudgments had been the cause. To Goering it had seemed that before, British fighter strength was nearly exhausted, and now it had bounced back again in an alarming way. The news was enough to sap his confidence in his staff and all his leaders. He asked Galland why had it happened. Galland could not tell him why, but he could tell his commander what had happened, and to his knowledge, British fighter strength seemed as great as ever, and British pilot morale extremely high.

The Luftwaffe came back in great strength on September 28, another fine day, to London and the Solent. The tactic was slightly changed: smaller bomber forces massively escorted by fighters. This made the odds more favorable, but the Luftwaffe lost another sixteen planes, as did the RAF that day.

The next day, September 29, the Germans returned once more, in the daytime to the south and east, but at night once more to London and Liverpool. Activity was slighter, and both sides lost five planes.

On September 30 the Luftwaffe staged another big daylight raid, this time escorting the bomber contingent with even more fighters.

The day began with the usual signs of a big buildup over the Pas de Calais, the sudden appearance of many tiny dots on the radar screen, milling about and waiting as more dots appeared and then forming up like a swarm of flies and heading north. Then came the shooting down of a German weather plane, a Ju-88 downed over North Devon.

By eight-thirty in the morning, the observers in Kent and Sussex were reporting that they sighted large formations of enemy aircraft through the scattered cloud cover.

At Group 11 headquarters at Uxbridge, Air Vice Marshal Park had a hunch that what was happening above was a feint by the Germans to bring his fighters up and that behind were coming even more fighters to attack the British planes in the air and on the ground. So he did not take the bait. The fighters stayed put on the ground, waiting for the bombers.

At nine-thirty the bombers began to come over, Ju-88s, unescorted. Air Marshal Park had 150 fighters ready to put into the air, and up they went, to meet the German bombers. At around ten o'clock that morning the British counterattack began—Spitfires and Hurricanes. Not long afterward several squadrons of Me-109s joined the fight and the hunting became more dangerous, but before they came, a dozen Ju-88s had crashed, and the others had dispersed their bombs over the countryside and headed home.

In the west that day General Sperrle's *Luftflotte* 3 had sent another raid against Bristol, aiming for the aircraft factory and the one at Yeovil. Erpro 210 was again involved, but this time the going was not easy. Five squadrons of Hurricanes and Spitfires met the Me-110s and the Heinkel bombers, and they did not achieve their objective but scattered bombs around the town of Sherborne.

What was apparent was that the radar and the operations network had recovered fully by this time and the operations centers were functioning smoothly, getting better every day. The evening saw another night raid on London that was a little less disastrous, but for the day the Germans lost forty-eight aircraft to the twenty fighters lost by the RAF. Erpro 210, the crack precision bombing unit, sent nineteen Me-110s against the aircraft factory north of Bristol, but this time they encountered the British fighters and four of the bombers were shot down, including the squadron leader.

After this negative day, Goering had to admit that the tactics had failed. Field Marshal Kesselring agreed. ''Because our losses were too high,'' he said, ''because we didn't have enough fighters to escort the bombers,'' they must stop raiding in the daylight hours. Kesselring's subordinates endorsed the idea heartily. There had once been a rule that the Luftwaffe should not lose more than one fighter to five of the enemy, but this had gone by the boards early in the Battle of Britain, and now the losses were much too great to bear. General Sperrle seemed to have the best conception of Britain's fighter production capacity, which had, in fact, surpassed that of the Luftwaffe. He and his staff looked at the situation, and although they could not at this time tell Goering, they suspected that the losses they had suffered would not be made up by production during the course of the war. There would be no more massive daylight raids, a tacit admission that the strength of British fighter command had not been breached.

But Goering had not given up on his promise to defeat the British in the air. He now ordered that a third of the fighter squadrons be converted to fighter bomber squadrons. They would carry the war to the enemy, each fighter bomber carrying a five-hundred-pound bomb that it would deliver before engaging the British fighters.

At the headquarters of General Theo Osterkamp, the commander of the German fighters of *Luftflotte* 2, the demand was greeted with derision and despair. A fighter burdened with a bomb was no longer a fighter, nor was it a bomber, but a flying monstrosity that would be prey for the Hurricanes and Spitfires. General Osterkamp complained to General Jeschonnek, who was Goering's administrator, but Jeschonnek, who agreed, could do nothing.

"It is a direct order from the führer," he said. Even Goering can do nothing to stop it. "Hitler thinks that the British are about to collapse, and the more bombs we can drop, the better."

For that reason, on October 1 the Luftwaffe's behavior changed remarkably. Years after, the war historians would say that the Battle of Britain ended on September 15, or on September 30 with the failure of these massive German efforts. But in 1940 Britain had no such conception of victory, nor was it certain to the British that the German invasion was not imminent. The British were in no way cognizant of the German plans, and only dimly of the German difficulties. They knew after the end of September that the invasion was going to be delayed, because the invasion fleet had been dispersed, but they also knew that spring was coming and that the invasion might well be mounted then. And since the Battle of Britain went on, on the sea, under the sea, and in the air, they continued to be alert and to prepare to resist invasion.

The new German strategy, ordered by Hitler, was to increase the bombing, by making fighters into bombers. So as of October 1, every night but one in October, the bombers came, under cover of darkness, an average of 150 per night, to haunt the streets of London, and with them came the fighter bombers carrying their bombs, and above all were the Me-109 fighters to protect the raids.

Night after night they came, and night after night the air raid wardens and the antiaircraft gunners were down there watching and waiting, the wardens to direct people to shelters, to call out the fire trucks, to help the rescue crews dig people out of the wreckage of their houses and their buildings.

On October 1 the Germans lost six planes and the British lost four fighters. The next night the German losses were higher—ten aircraft to a single British fighter. On the night of October 3 a single German Ju-88 bombed the Dehaviland factory at Hatfield, but there was little other damage and the Luftwaffe lost nine aircraft again to one British loss.

On October 4 Hitler met with Mussolini. He still talked about the invasion of Britain, which now had to be put off until spring, but he had convinced himself that the only thing to prevent the Luftwaffe from achieving its total victory was the absence of five consecutive days of good weather in these last weeks. Again that day, the Germans attacked in fog and rain, and lost a dozen planes in doing it to only three planes from the British side. On that day on the other side of the Channel, Air Vice Marshal Park issued new instructions to his sector controller and squadron commanders. They were to put their planes in the air when they had the first alert and to get them up to twenty-five thousand feet, to await further instructions.

On October 5 Erpro 210, the pinpoint Me-110 bomber squadron, made a heavy attack on a newly completed fighter field at West Malling, and ran into difficulties with the RAF's Squadron 303, which shot down four of the Me-110s, including the plane of the new commander of the unit, and damaged two more Me-110s so badly that they crash-landed in the Pas de Calais area.

On October 7 Reichsmarschal Goering redefined the German objectives in the bombing of Britain to be the "progressive and complete annihilation" of London, the paralyzing of Britain's war production and civil life, and the terrorization and privation of the civil population of London and the provinces. It would be done with night bombers, there would be no more wasteful daylight raids. And the provinces would begin to get their share.

On October 8 Air Vice Marshal Park issued orders for standing patrols, to be ready at all times for these high-altitude intruders. It was an expensive business in terms of fuel consumption, but it helped the defenders find their enemies in time.

The raid on the night of October 9 was spectacular. Raiders were over Wales in the west, the Midlands, Liverpool, the southwest part of England, and the northeast. The outskirts of London got the worst bombing that night. And that night the Germans used many incendiaries, which would fall often in long strings covering a mile or more.

After two months of bombing, by the middle of October Britons had come to grips with the bombing in their own ways. One widespread idea was that if you had suffered a near miss, you were not likely to have another. In other words, you had paid your dues. Along with this came the idea that no place was ever hit twice. Of course, there were exceptions, but that is what people believed, and it gave them a sort of comfort to believe.

But what was happening in October was not nice in another sense. The Germans had improved their Me-109s with a more powerful engine and long-range gas tanks, so that it could carry a five-hundred-pound bomb to London. These aircraft came over from the Pas de Calais in a more or less steady stream at night, and they dropped their bombs on London. These bombs killed and wounded a large number of people, as in Piccadilly Circus on October 12.

That day, CBS correspondent Edward R. Murrow went down to the mouth of the Thames, where he had witnessed the start of the bombing of London in September, to see what changes had come. He found the green and white pub across the road from his favorite haystack had been blown up, but the countryside had not changed much. The haystack remained, just as it was on the night he had sought shelter there when the bombers were streaming up the Thames Estuary, a month before, so long, long ago.

The apple crop had been picked and the hops harvested. Only a few planes came over, and he saw no fires up the river. In the morning he drove to Folkestone, and found very little damage. Then he went on to Dover for lunch. He saw the town still thriving, although his favorite hotel had been smashed, but otherwise the town looked much the same.

He drove on to Canterbury to see what had happened there. The Germans had announced that Canterbury was going to be a prime target. He found that the raid they bragged about had killed five people and knocked down a few buildings, but the cathedral still stood. While he was there that afternoon, an air raid was announced by the sirens. All he could see of it was a handful of British fighters, visible by their contrails, high in the sky, swinging in a circle above the cathedral.

Late in the afternoon Murrow drove back to London on the south side, near the docks. He noted that the damage had been severe there, particularly to small houses. The poor people who lived near the docks had been the ones to suffer most. And he was reminded more of the war than he had been all day, for hundreds of people were already moving toward the shelters.

That day Hitler issued a new directive about the air war. It came in the form of a memo from Field Marshal Keitel, chief of staff of OKW. "The führer has decided," it said, "that from now on until spring, preparations for Operation Sea Lion shall be continued solely for the purpose of maintaining political and military pressure on England.

"Should the invasion be reconsidered in the spring or early summer of 1941, orders for a renewal of operational readiness will be issued latter. In the meantime, military conditions for a later invasion are to be improved."

It was a new sort of air war, designed to carry out Hitler's plan of terrorizing London. On October 15 a single Me-109 came through the barrage and dropped a bomb on Victoria Station, killing many and wounding many other Britons. But that was not all. That night more than four hundred German bombers were over London, doing their damage.

The defenders had a new problem: The Me-109s came over at altitudes up to thirty-three thousand feet and dropped their bombs from that altitude. That meant the fighters had to climb high and fast to intercept them before they reached London, and only the Spitfires could reach this altitude. Since the Spitfires comprised only about a third of the British fighter force, the Germans operated with a new advantage. The pressures on the fighter force grew high again, and it was almost a replay of the August and September strain. On several days the number of Me-109 sorties exceeded a thousand.

By October 17 the people of London celebrated a sort of a watch point: forty days and forty nights of air raids. The air raid was "old hat" now. The women at the Lyons Corner House in Marble Arch were no longer talking about the bombing. As they came off duty, the boyfriends were hanging about the staff entrance, to meet the women and take them out. They went to the pubs and to milk bars, and they walked along the streets when the bombs were going off. The women sometimes thought of stopping and going into a shelter for the night with their young men, but they knew that would create a fearful ruckus at home, so they usually did not, but braved their way home through the flashing and the noise.

The conclusion of reporter Tom Harrisson was that the six Nippy girls had adjusted, managing to pick up their main interests, a job, a boyfriend, the cinema, and pubs, West End trips to see how the toffs live. They did all these things in spite of the bombs.

And if one read the newspaper advertisements of these days, and not the news stories about the Blitz, one would scarcely know that there had been a change brought by the war. Hair tonic to take away that gray, a substance that cleans hands as well as pots, advertisements for cough medicines, coffee, and shoe polish, and paste for false teeth. Auto dealers would still send cars out on road tests (what happened if a road test car was hit by a bomb?). There were advisers to help fill out income tax. Nerve tonic that was "guaranteed" to work. An advertisement for greyhound racing at the big sports arena. Cocoa at very favorable prices. In Glasgow *Gone With the Wind* was ending its twenty-first week.

But there were also advertisements that reflected the war. The ad for a substance that made the weekly single egg of the ration into scrambled eggs for two. An ad to "fly with the Royal Air Force." A remedy for "shelter sickness." A whiskey ad for a brand that was "invaluable in any emergency." And a clothier who offered suits that would survive the Blitz, and twelve months to pay—which was certainly a confident tribute to the indestructibility of the human spirit.

# CHAPTER 14

# *The Scene Shifts*

In the middle of October, the eighteenth to be precise, Reichsmarschal Goering stopped to give praise to his fighter pilots for inflicting terrible losses on the British enemy, and his bomber pilots for having reduced the British government to fear and trembling.

It was true that RAF fighter command's loss of pilots over the last three months had been serious, but the fact was that there were more pilots and more aircraft in mid-October than there had been in July. There was not an iota of truth in the second claim, and the two were made in an attempt to succor the falling morale of the Luftwaffe, which had not only suffered serious losses during the Battle of Britain, but had been reviled, insulted, and abused by Goering himself. Hitler's interference in such matters as forcing fighter pilots to become bomb deliverers had not helped, either.

From this point on, the weather worsened and would continue to worsen, and it had to be felt in the air campaign particularly. On October 16 it was cloudy, and the Germans put up a steady stream of bombers, losing thirteen planes to the RAF's three. The next day it rained off and on, the raids were generally the same, about 150 bombers, with a Luftwaffe loss of fifteen to three RAF planes. Britain was largely hidden by fog, but the raiders came anyway and lost another fifteen aircraft. The RAF lost four fighters.

111

Clouds covered Britain on October 19, but the bombers came, and lost five. October 20 was also cloudy, and to take advantage of poor visibility, the high-flying fighter bombers with their five-hundred-pound bombs reverted to mass attacks, following the Hitler logic that every bomb delivered, no matter how or when, added to the terror under which the British people were suffering. The change cost the Luftwaffe a lot of aircraft, fourteen, mostly fighter bombers, this day.

On October 23 fog really cut back on operations and so the Germans lost only six aircraft, while the RAF lost none. The next day the Germans were experimenting again. They raided Glasgow as well as London, at night, of course, in a small, experimental raid. In the last few days, air crashes because of the weather had cost the Germans nearly as many planes as had RAF and antiaircraft gun action, but Hitler's orders were explicit, the pressure must be kept on Britain, and so the raids were made. On October 24 the Luftwaffe's results were dismal, but they still lost eight aircraft.

Mussolini was angry and his prestige hurt by the British air raids on northern Italian cities, and eager to participate fully in the battle against Britain, and he offered both submarines and air forces to his ally Hitler. On the surface, the offer seemed worth accepting; the Italians had the largest submarine force in Europe and a very large air force. But the Italian submarines were not built to withstand the sort of weather that U-boat men were used to in the North Atlantic, and their methods of operation did not mesh with those of Admiral Doenitz and his U-boat force. Also, many of the Italian aircraft were far inferior to the German. The Italians joined in the Battle of Britain on both levels, but when they raided Harwich on October 25, the results were dismal, and they and the Germans lost twenty aircraft.

October 26 and 27 were cloudy with showers; the Germans flew raids on both days, attacking seven airfields and continuing the fighter bomber raids. The bigger bombers were coming in with hit-and-run attacks by individual planes or in small groups. The British worked hard these two days, shooting down twenty-five enemy planes. On October 27 alone, fighter command flew off a thousand sorties.

Every day, every day, they came. On October 28 they

penetrated through cloud cover to bomb very inaccurately. On October 29 they staged another giant "circus."

The day dawned hazily, the mist drifting along in the light winds low above the ground. The early warnings brought the first squadron of Spitfires into the air at a quarter to eleven that morning. They climbed high, and the ground was soon lost beneath the haze, but at twenty thousand feet the sky was clear and blue, and soon the squadron leader spotted a formation of Me-109s crossing the coastline. A squadron of these were fighter bombers, carrying their five-hundred-pound bombs, and they headed for London while two squadrons of the Me-109s turned to the Spitfires to fight it out and protect the fighter bombers. Most of the fighter bombers were forced to jettison their bombs over the countryside, but two got through and dropped their bombs very close to Charing Cross railroad station.

A little later, about one hundred Me-109s appeared. They ran into five Spitfire squadrons at twenty-eight thousand feet and four Hurricane squadron's at twenty-two thousand feet. The Spitfires hit them high, and when the Me-109s maneuverd and lost altitude, the Hurricanes came in to chew at their flanks. The fighter bombers among the Me-109s jettisoned their bombs over the countryside, and raced back to the Channel, with several shot down. Of the fighter protection, eleven were shot down.

Still later in the day, Erpro 210 came along, its Me-110s seeking an airfield to attack. They were accompanied by some Me-109 fighter bombers. They chose North Weald and arrived just as two squadrons of Hurricanes were taking off. The German planes destroyed two planes in the takeoff process, and killed several ground personnel. But their squadron leader, Otto Hintze, was shot down and taken prisoner.

On the twenty-ninth the Italians came again, with fifteen bombers protected by their own fighter planes. The bombers faintly resembled the Heinkel 111, but there was something different about their configuration. They were escorted by seventy brightly colored biplane fighters, which the antiaircraft gunners said must have been left over from World War I. The Italians did not come far. They crossed the coast and came up the Kent countryside, but when the guns began to fire on them, they made a sharp right turn in one great formation, and moved back and out to sea, dropping a few bombs here and there. They had bombed England. That was the important matter. They had not accomplished anything and they had not lost any aircraft. It was a comic opera victory.

Three weeks later the Italians tried the act again, but on this second occasion they chose as a target Harwich, and ran into British fighters and antiaircraft guns. Thirteen bombers and biplane fighters were shot down.

During October the German attack had broadened to include Liverpool, Manchester, Birmingham, and other cities. By the end of that month thirteen thousand British civilians had been killed in the bombing, and twenty thousand seriously wounded.

There was no question of the attacks stopping. Hitler had decreed that the pressure was to be kept on until the spring weather would make the invasion possible again. Then, he said, he would make the decision—and the implication was that the fierce Battle of Britain, with the concentration on destroying the fighter capacity of England, would begin all over again.

Admiral Raeder said that the way to defeat England was to hit at her lifelines, to destroy her position in the Mediterranean, to continue and increase the submarine warfare, and to augment it with raids by the pocket battleships, battleships, and cruisers of the Germany navy. Hitler began to listen, and all these moves were in the German plan in the late fall of 1940.

Hitler, in fact, did not know what to do about an enemy that he had declared to be defeated but would not lie down. Therefore, the air war went on, although it was more and more clear that it was no longer directed at military targets but at the general population.

But in early November the Luftwaffe, mindful of Hitler's orders to keep the pressure on the British, decided that a new direction was in order. The attack on London had not kicked Britain into surrender, even though Winston Churchill said he feared the British capital would be reduced to one great pile of rubble before the war ended.

Therefore, something new was in order. The Luftwaffe

was also painfully aware that the British production of aircraft had not been significantly reduced by all their bombings. This was not strictly true—some of their raids, such as those on the Supermarine plant at Southampton, had been devastating—but the British had persevered and even increased aircraft production so that in the year 1940 it surpassed the production of fighter planes by the Germans.

The decision was made to broaden the base of the night air attacks and to begin hitting other industrial centers hard, to destroy British war production.

Toward the end of August, when the Germans began to switch over from daytime bombing to nighttime attacks, the RAF was ready with countermeasures for the Knickebein beam.

After the Knickebein beam had been located in June, a special RAF organization had been established to deal with it, No. 80 Wing with its headquarters at Radlett, north of London. Here were jammers, which would transmit a mush of noise on the Knickebein frequencies. But in reserve and nearly ready was a much more sophisticated device, called "aspirin" because it was to be an antidote to the headache of the Knickebeins. It consisted of high-powered equipment that transmitted a sound very much like the Knickebein sound, so much so that a German bomber flying along the Knickebein track would hear the Knickebein signal plus this superimposed dash, and he would think he had moved into the dash zone of overlapping beams and thus steer into the dot zone to bring the dots up in volume. In time the British would make this even more sophisticated so they could bend the beams, and thus steer the Germans off course, but for now they could only confuse them.

Knickebein came into play with the night bombing, or tried to. But the jamming was successful, and the story soon spread throught the Luftwaffe that the beam was jammed. Every pilot knew it, but nobody wanted to tell Marshal Goering, so he went blissfully for the next two months believing that Knickebein was leading his boys to victory.

In September the cryptographer at Bletchley came upon a new line of Enigma machine code traffic involving what was called the X-Apparatus. It was a new system of beams, and posed a new series of problems for Dr. Jones and the experts on Knickebein.

The Germans had great hopes for their new X beams. General Milch told Marshal Goering that if night attacks were to be successful, the beam system would have to be perfected, and a special unit *Kampf Gruppe* 100 was working on the problem with special aircraft and special systems.

To counter this new sort of beam attack, the British needed to decode Enigma messages in time to find out where the *Kampf Gruppe* 100 attack was scheduled for that night and then have the jamming system ready to beam there, and the fighters ready to go there. The problem was that the orders to the beam stations were issued only two or three hours before the attack. But the British codebreakers persisted, and one October night they managed to do this, and thereafter to repeat the performance one night in three. Thus the RAF then would know the place of attack, the time of attack, the line of approach of the bombers, their ground speed, and their altitude.

But the Germans were also becoming more proficient in the use of their several X beam stations—at least six different X beams—near Cherbourg, Calais, and Brest. By setting and resetting their beams, *Kampf Gruppe* 100 could attack two targets in succession on the same night. And they would: Birmingham and Coventry on November 4, Coventry and Liverpool on November 5, and Liverpool and Birmingham on November 8. Sometimes the KGr100 pilots acted as pathfinders for other units.

One thing was certain as the autumn deepened: the Germans were bombing with more accuracy, except when the British could intercept and confuse their beams.

On November 10 Dr. Jones in London received a teleprint of a decoded Enigma message to the X beam stations, which had been sent the previous day. It was unusual, because it specified operations against three targets, given numbers 51, 52, and 53. It gave the beam settings, so Dr. Jones could figure out that 51 was Wolverhampton, 52 was Birmingham, and 53 was Coventry.

Also on November 3 the messages between *Luftflotte* 2, which was Marshal Kesselring's headquarters, and the subordinate organizations began to increase, which meant some sort of change was in the air. The change, although they did not know it in London, was to be a broadening of the Blitz to encompass many more target cities. On November 11 came a long Enigma message concerning a major air operation which was codenamed Moonlight Sonata. KGr 100 was to be involved, which meant that the beams would be employed. Four targets, A, B, C, and D, were involved.

Dr. Jones again had access to intelligence from a Luftwaffe prisoner who said that the attacks would be made between November 15 and November 20 on Birmingham and Coventry. But the air intelligence people thought the attacks would be in the south of England, and so Dr. Jones was overruled in his attempts to have the RAF concentrate its defenses in the Midlands and the north. He pointed to the unusual threat to Birmingham, Coventry, and Wolverhampton, but nobody was listening.

On Thursday evening, November 14, 1940, after two months of the intensive bombing of London, the Luftwaffe decided on a different ploy. London was a difficult target because the fighter fields were nearby, and because the concentration of searchlights and antiaircraft guns made it a dangerous task to try to penetrate that air space above the city.

On that night of November 14, the German attention was focused on the city of Coventry, a metropolis of 250,000 people, middle-sized and located in the Midlands. As a military target, all that could be said really was that Coventry was the home of a number of engineering industries. It was also the site of a fourteenth-century cathedral.

Why Coventry?

In the first place, it was an important city in the British defense effort. At the time of Dunkirk, Prime Minister Churchill had characterized it in a secret paper as second only to Liverpool in importance. Its twenty-one major factories were deemed essential to the war effort. But in spite of this feeling in high places, nothing had been done to prepare or protect Coventry in case of attack.

The Germans again were trying to terrorize the British, but in a different way. They had failed to strike terror into the hearts of Londoners, so now they would take the war to "the people" in the countryside. That was what Coventry really meant, the sacrifice of any pretense of aiming at purely military targets.

On that night of November 14, 450 Luftwaffe bombers struck at Coventry, dropping five hundred tons of high-explosive bombs. This was twice as much high explosive dropped on this one little area as the total bombs dropped on any single similarly-sized section of London in the past month. And the high explosives were not all of it by far. The Germans also dropped nearly nine hundred incendiary canisters on Coventry, bombs that split open and spread their fires.

Coventry had thirty-two heavy antiaircraft guns and fifty-six barrage balloons to protect it. That night the Germans slipped through the defenses, and the fighters did not appear in any force. The weather was fine, and the RAF put up 125 fighters, but they did not find the bombers that night; only seven RAF pilots even saw the enemy, and only two opened fire. Only one of the 450 bombers was shot down.

It was the largest single air raid and the most concentrated yet launched against any point in Britain. As the Germans knew it would be, the raid was completely unanticipated, and not very many things had been done to protect the people if the air raid came.

In September the government had warned about bombing and suggested the movement of children from the cities. About fifteen thousand children were eligible, but only three thousand of them had gone.

In the event, more than 550 people were killed and nearly 900 were injured. As planned, the effect was truly devastating in a physical sense.

The government and the civil defense people had advised the evacuation of cities, not just London. At Newcastle, 70 percent of the children had been evacuated, and at Manchester and Liverpool, more than 60 percent had gone. But at Coventry only 20 percent of the children had been moved out, and after a month or so, when nothing happened, most of them had come back. Then suddenly, in one night, the whole city core had disappeared. The cathedral stood there, gutted; at each end, the frames of the great windows without any glass, and in between, a wasteland of rubble, bricks, parts of pillars, steel girders to reinforce the work of the fourteenth- and fifteenth-century workmen, tombs, and memorial tablets.

In the town, a third of all the houses were either gone or uninhabitable.

Everywhere, what had been order and streets and buildings was now bricks and stones, and mortar and jagged concrete pieces, boards, snakes of wire hanging from broken poles and twisted pipes jutting up from below the debris, twisted sheets of iron roofing and aluminim and wood.

Two hospitals were among the buildings badly bombed, although, of course, they bore on their roofs the big red cross of the lifesaving institutions, so as not to be mistaken for any of the twenty-one big factories in Coventry.

Next morning as people picked their way out of the rubble and moved off and as the rescue workers and police and wardens poked among the debris for survivors, the city was still smoking and the metal was still red-hot.

When dawn came and the wind had blown the smoke away, the town officials gazed around them, awestruck, and apparently paralyzed. As Tom Harrisson, the recorder of the Blitz for the BBC, noted in a later book:

"The overwhelming dominant feeling on Friday was the feeling of utter helplessness. The tremendous impact of the previous night had left people practically speechless. And it made them feel impotent. There was no role for the civilian. Ordinary people had no idea of what they should do. And this helplessness and impotence only accelerated depression."

The police and the national officials half expected a renewal of the attack the following night, but if the Germans had intended to make a solitary objective of Coventry, their signals got mixed. More likely was that observation the next morning showed such devastation that the Germans believed (as did many people of the city) that Coventry was "finished."

London sent down some experts on that first day, and they like most other people, waited for the other shoe to fall that second night. But nothing happened. The Blitz switched back to London with another two hundred bombers or so, and the air over the Midlands was quiet and serene. Coventry people began to look more calm. Even those who had suffered great loss, like the woman who ran a little milk bar, assumed that same calm in twenty-four hours that was already associated with London. Her husband had been killed in the raid, and lay buried beneath the rubble of what had been a surface air raid shelter that had taken a direct hit. She mentioned this quite casually as she apologized for the slow service in her establishment.

In a day or two, six hundred soldiers showed up to begin clearing, dynamiting, and tearing down the rubble of the buildings. Soon the number of soldiers had doubled. At first the people moved out, going anywhere just to get away. The nearby towns and villages were inundated with refugees. Only two of the rest centers—St Thomas's and St. Barbara's—were functioning. But in ten days people were complaining and worrying about the future, but they were back.

Everyone expected a new raid. They watched the German observation planes come over, obviously taking pictures of the rubble and the sentinel wreckage of the cathedral.

But the Germans did not come back. By November 25 Coventry was beginning to assume signs of life. The damage was great, but it was not impossible. Most of the twenty-one factories could carry on some production at least. Within five days most industrial production was restored. The Germans certainly did not know that. They were the victim of their own propaganda, which boasted that Coventry had been destroyed. Had their photo analysts looked carefully at the photos they took (most of which centered on the shattered cathedral as the symbol of devastation), they might have seen the antlike recovery proceeding in the city. But they did not. It was many months before the Luftwaffe returned to Coventry, and never again did the German air force devote so much attention to any city but London. So the Coventry raid stood out as a symbol of what might have been (another night or two and the city would indeed have been finished) and the German inability to stick with a job until it was done, one of the graces that surely saved England in the Battle of Britain.

It is common to consider the Battle of Britain as the air war alone, because the air war was central to the German hope of bringing Britain to surrender quickly. But the fact is that the air war was not fought in a vacuum. When it began in the summer of 1940, the ports and shipping were major targets of the Luftwaffe. The Luftwaffe was also supposed to coordinate its efforts with those of the U-boat service (although they never did do so satisfactorily). And also, the German warships were involved in this multifaceted effort called the Battle of Britain. By October 1940 the pocket battleship *Scheer* was ready for service. She left Germany on October 27 and headed into the Denmark Strait north of Iceland. Breaking out, she was in the Atlantic. She was followed a few weeks later by the eight-inch gun cruiser *Hipper*. The British had withdrawn their battleship escorts from the Atlantic convoys in order to reinforce the Mediterranean, and this was to be the hunting ground of the big ships as well as the U-boats. The *Scheer* in these wintry days was looking for a convoy that left Halifax on October 27. On November 5 Captain Krancke's aircraft found eight ships in the southeast and he started to pursue them. In early afternoon of that day he sighted one ship, the *Mopan*, which he sank by gunfire. At 5:40 P.M. he came upon the masts of the Convoy HX84, which consisted of thirty-seven ships. His way was blocked by the armed merchant cruiser *Jervis Bay*, which carried old-fashioned six-inch guns. The *Jervis Bay* opened fire, and the *Scheer* opened fire, but the merchant cruisers's shells fell short, so it was a one-sided battle ending in the sinking of the *Jervis Bay*, but the escape of the convoy. The *Scheer* pursued, but the ships scattered and she was able to sink only five of them before they escaped in the darkness of night.

The *Scheer* then went to the West Indies, where she was not notably successful in finding ships, and in the spring of 1941 returned to Kiel, having been five months abroad and sinking sixteen ships.

This surface raiding was one part of the Battle of Britain, the U-boat work was another—all of it aimed at the same end, to keep the pressure on Britain and prepare the way for the invasion of the spring.

The U-boat threat really worried Winston Churchill at least as much as the air battle at its most dangerous point, those first two weeks when Goering nearly knocked out Britain's air defenses.

Churchill said this:

"A far greater danger was added to these problems. The only thing that ever really frightened me during the war was the U-boat peril. Invasion, I thought, even before the air battle, would fail. After the air victory (September, 1940) it was a good battle for us. We could drown and kill this horrible foe in circumstances favorable to us, and, as he evidently realized, bad for him. It was the kind of battle which, in the cruel conditions of war, one ought to be content to fight. But now our lifeline even across the broad oceans and especially in the entrances to the island, was endangered. I was even more anxious about this battle than I had been about the glorious air fight . . ."

As if to emphasize the problems Britain faced in this difficult winter, the U-boats were proving successful with a new tactic highly suitable for the five-hundred-ton Atlantic boats. It involved attacking on the surface, usually at night, hitting a convoy, moving through it, and then running off at high speed. Several convoys were badly cut up in October and November. But the U-boat catastrophes and the surface ship catastrophes came in batches, while in this wintry time, the air war came night after night with grinding regularity.

# CHAPTER 15

# The New Sea War

By the autumn of 1940, in conjunction with the bombing of British ports and industrial installations in the Blitz, Admiral Doenitz stepped up his sea war against the British, who had been sorely hurt by the loss of many destroyers in the Dunkirk evacuation, and thus were short of patrol vessels and convoy escorts.

At first that summer, the U-boat campaign was turned to paving the way for the expected invasion—Operation Sea Lion—and that expectation continued with one delay after another until October.

During the month of September, the air forces and U-boat forces were augmented by E-boats, which began major operations off the east coast against British shipping. The majority of sinkings of the U-boats was occurring off the Irish coast. Something new was added, the night U-boat attack. Convoy HX72 was successfully attacked by a U-boat wolf pack, and twelve ships, or seventy-eight thousand tons of shipping, were sunk, seven of them by one U-boat.

During the month of October the British lost 103 ships for 443,000 tons, about a quarter of it by air attack from Luftwaffe planes, and most of the rest by U-boats. Convoys were provided with escorts to a farther point about three hundred miles west of Ireland. The Canadians gave similar cover for a similar distance on their side. But there remained that vast expanse of mid-Atlantic, and there were too few escorts to take the convoys through the area safely. By this time the wolf pack had become a definite factor in submarine attack.

In mid-October, eleven U-boats were operating in the North Atlantic. They carried their part of the Battle of Britain by sinking thirty-nine ships. To increase the protection, Prime Minister Churchill had to make a difficult decision: to dismantle part of the antiinvasion force, even though he did not know for sure that the Germans would not try an invasion. It was a gravely calculated risk, made possible by the RAF success thus far in the Battle of Britain.

But what the British did have going for them in the fall of 1940 was an increase of activity by coastal command, which made the entrance and exit into such bases as Lorient a difficult matter.

Still, the U-boats were contributing their share to the attempted destruction of Britain's power to make war, and that summer and fall the U-boats held the upper hand. U-boat Captain Otto Kretschmer had developed a new technique to counteract the British asdic sound detection system: the night attack on the surface conducted at high speed, running through a convoy, scattering torpedoes, and then escaping at high speed on the surface before the escorts knew what had hit their charges.

In August and September as the air war raged above Britain, British losses at sea climbed above three hundred thousand tons per month, and as the year came to its end, the shipping losses for the period since the real war had begun in France topped the two-million ton mark.

In those two months the Germans lost only four U-boats. *U-51* was sunk by a British submarine. *U-25* hit a mine in British waters. *U-102* also hit a mine, and *U-57* was rammed by a Norwegian freighter she was attacking in the Baltic Sea. The score, then, was highly favorable to the U-boats, and it had Prime Minister Churchill worried.

But coastal command was becoming organized. In October, when the *U-31* went out from Lorient, she had to dive four times to escape British aircraft in the area south of St. George's Channel. This was something new to the Germans, and they were not yet used to it. Soon enough they would become so.

In the autumn the Italians entered the Battle of Britain, in the air and under the sea. The Italian fleet numbered one hundred submarines; they could put eighty boats to sea immediately, which was more than four times the number that Doenitz had operational. On paper their strength was so alarming that Prime Minister Churchill spoke in the cabinet meeting of abandoning the whole eastern Mediterranean.

The Italians were particularly angry because the British had conducted a number of bombing raids against northern Italian cities that summer and fall. Italian submarine commanders came to Germany and France and went on patrol with Doenitz's senior U-boat skippers to learn the ropes, and then a number of Italian submarines set up at the new U-boat port of Bordeaux. They, too, began to sink ships, but what became apparent quite early was that Italian submarines were not designed to operate in rough North Atlantic winter waters. Their conning towers were too big, for one thing, and they shipped too much water into the boat in rough seas. Nor were the Italians trained in the Doenitz operational fashion, in which he maintained direct control of their activity at all times.

The Germans tried hard and the Italians tried hard to accommodate themselves to one another. Doenitz brought a number of Italian captains to Wilhelmshaven; they took courses in German, and they went to school to learn German methods. But between October 10 and November 30 the Italian submarines sank only one ship of 5,000 tons, having put in 243 submarine days at sea, while the German U-boats had sunk eighty ships totalling 450,000 tons in 378 days at sea. The Italians improved on their score that winter, but still the experiment was not a great success and it was soon abandoned. The Italians went back to their own activity, in the middle and South Atlantic and the Mediterranean, and they operated in their own way.

In the rough weather of winter 1940, the submarine sinkings decreased, just as did the bombing raids over Britain, shipping losses falling below the three-hundred-thousand-ton mark. But the war at sea was a serious matter in conjunction with the Luftwaffe. Also, Goering had promised cooperation with Doentiz's submarine arm, and he tried to live up to the promises by assigning several squadrons of Dornier bombers and flying boats to become the "eyes" of the submarine fleet. When this program worked, it worked well, and several British convoys were badly hit when they were first bombed by Luftwaffe planes, which then reported on position, course, and speed, and the submarines came next, to take more victims. The Germans had developed an eighteen-inch aerial torpedo, which carried 440 pounds of explosive, with a range of twenty-seven hundred yards and a speed of thirty-five knots.

In the fall of 1940 the Third *Staffel* of *Geschwader* 406, flying Heinkel 115 and Heinkel 59 bombers, was based on the inner harbor at Stavanger, and began conducting torpedo attacks against British shipping in the North Sea, mostly at night. The aircraft were painted black, which made them extremely hard to see. They approached shipping, usually lone ships, and came down to a level of fifty feet above the sea, to attack. As of the end of December 1940, the British had not yet discovered these aircraft, and the losses they caused by torpedoing were attributed to other causes.

The U-boats continued to cause serious trouble in the British supply situation. That fall the British listed seventeen U-boat commanders who had been awarded the Knight's Cross of the Iron Cross, an award given for the sinking of many ships, usually one hundred thousand tons. They included Guenther Prien, whose *U-47* had sunk the battleship *Royal Oak* in 1939, Herbert Schultze, Otto Schuhart, Otto Kretschmer, who had devised the night surface attack on convoys, and Hans Jenisch, whose exploits in *U-32* had amazed the British.

The exploits of *U-32* in that autumn of 1940 indicate the new pressure being exerted against the British in connection with the air battle. Lieutenant Jenisch had just come back from a war cruise to Lorient, the new base in France, arriving on September 8, but because of the pressure on the U-boat force to perform, the *U-32* went out again only ten days later on her seventh war cruise.

She left Lorient again on September 18, and was accompanied by a minesweeper as far as the entrance to the harbor. Thereafter she was on her own and proceeded to her operational area, several hundred miles to the west, in the Atlantic. Other boats were sent to the north in Doenitz's attempt to close off the Northern Approaches to the British shipping.

The activities of the U-boats were closely controlled by Doenitz and his staff. In the operations room stood a chart table not unlike that in the fighter command headquarters in Britain, a table that divided the whole Western world into grids. At any given time, by moving markers around the board, Doenitz knew exactly where his submarines were operating, and he controlled them through high-speed, high-powered radio transmissions. Like all the other successful captains, Skipper Jenisch responded quickly to Doenitz's orders. This was the essence of the U-boat success.

The *U-32* carried eleven torpedoes, five in the tubes and ready to fire, and six spares. At 5:50 on the morning of September 22 the ship attacked a convoy that had been discovered for the U-boats by Kaptaenleutnant Schepke, another of the "star captains." She first attacked the SS *Collegian* on the surface with gunfire. The steamship turned its stern to the submarine and opened fire with its deck gun. The U-boat fired twenty-five rounds, but did not come closer than two hundred yards to the ship. The ship fired ten rounds from its deck gun, and the last shell was so close that Schepke broke off the engagement and dived.

The steamer then began signaling that she had been attacked by a submarine, and the U-boat fired a torpedo, which missed. Seeing the gun flashes, the captain of the destroyer HMS *Lowestoff*, which was fifteen miles away from the action, turned his vessel and came up to the scene, with three other escorts, HMS *Skate*, HMS *Shikari*, and HMS *Heartsease*. After fifty minutes of search, HMS *Lowestoff* had an asdic contact, fourteen hundred yards away. She altered course to close, but as sometimes happened with the cranky asdic, the contact was lost when altering course. She regained contact and came in to attack. At 9:20 in the morning *Lowestoff* attacked, dropped six depth charges at 250-, 350-, and 500-foot depths. Again, as sometimes happened, contact was lost in the concussion of the attacks, and although she continued to search with other escorts, the contact was not regained. The U-boat had dived to 180 feet and then moved westward out of range.

In the next few days, the *U-32* sank the SS *Corrientes* and the Empire *Ocelot*. The latter ship was traveling in ballast—which meant empty—from England to America to pick up supplies when she was sunk off the Irish coast. The crew took to the boats after a torpedo disabled their ship and she began to sink. They saw the U-boat surface and shell the sinking ship, and then they saw the ship sink.

The submarine also sank the SS *Darcoila*, traveling alone, out of Milford Haven to America, and the Dutch ship *Hanlerwijk*. Skipper Jenisch brought his submarine up very close to the sinking Dutch ship because he wanted to read the name on the stern—too close, because he collided with the ship, damaging the U-boat's bow. But she was able to make Lorient, which she did on October 3, to receive congratulations for a successful cruise, in which she had sunk forty-three thousand tons of British shipping.

The crew went home to leave to Germany, and on October 10 Jenisch was decorated with the Knight's insignia of the Iron Cross. He was now one of the "stars" of the U-boat fleet. Because of the nature of the Battle of Britain, enormous publicity was given to this event by Propaganda Minister Goebbels's orders.

In the third week of October, the crew was together again at Lorient and they sailed on October 24, again accompanied by a minesweeper.

The *U-32* moved out very quickly to the edge of the Western Approaches, in the drive to break down British morale, and she was soon in her cruising area.

This time she and other U-boats in the area were operating with the Luftwaffe. On October 26 Luftwaffe bombers found the big liner *Empress of Britain* and set her afire, but did not sink her. She was dead in the water fifty miles off the northwest coast of Ireland when tugs found her and two destroyers came to escort her home. Jenisch had the news of the *Empress of Britain* from Doenitz.

Skipper Jenisch took the U-boat to the path of the *Empress of Britain*, waited while the two destroyers zigzagged past, and then when the *Empress of Britain* under tow came by, he surfaced and fired three torpedoes at her from eighteen hundred yards. Two of the torpedoes exploded on the port side of the ship. The *Empress of Britain* was immediately enveloped in a large cloud of steam as Jenisch took the submarine away on the surface at high speed. When the steam evaporated, the sea was clear. The liner had sunk.

On October 30 the U-boat sighted the British merchant ship *Balzac* off the Irish coast, and at noon she fired a torpedo, which missed, and the torpedo exploded on the starboard side of the vessel about fifty yards away from her.

The *Balzac* reported that she was under attack by a submarine. Two destroyers, the HMS *Highlander* and HMS *Harvester*, were searching for Convoy SC8, which they were supposed to pick up and escort back to England. The radio officer of the steamer heard pulsing sounds, and the ship's captain concluded that they might be followed by the submarine, which was indeed the case. The *Balzac* then ran into several rain squalls to confuse the U-boat if there was one. The *Harvester* arrived at about 5:40 in the afternoon, and her captain interrogated the captain of the *Balzac* about the attack and then informed the captain of *Highlander*.

Meanwhile the *U-32* had submerged and trailed the *Balzac* all afternoon. Captain Jenisch brought the *U-32* to periscope depth, saw two destroyers and the ship, and ducked back down. But the destroyers moved away, and then Jenisch pursued the merchant ship while submerged. The radio officer of the steamer once again reported that he heard sounds like those of an underwater electric motor.

"Rot," said the captain of the ship. "That is our own noise."

Submarine skipper Jenisch seemed to have forgotten the presence of the two British destroyers in the area. That was not really the case; the sounds of the two destroyers were masked from the U-boat by the noise of the engines of the merchant ship, which was much louder. And the merchant ship was between the submarine and the two destroyers as they moved along, so Jenisch did not know they were still very close by. At 6:12 P.M. the captain of the *Harvester* came up around the *Balzac* to her port bow, and a thousand yards away he had a contact. Before he could do anything about it, the submarine periscope came up, sticking out of the water two feet and clearly visible.

Jenisch raised his periscope and was shocked to see the *Harvester* right on him. He dropped the periscope and crash-dived, only eighty yards off the destroyer's port beam.

The skipper of the *Harvester* signaled SSSSSSSS—submarine in sight—and ordered the ship hard astern to port, full ahead starboard, to swing around to ram the U-boat. But as the ship turned, the U-boat came inside the destroyer's turning circle, and so the captain of the British ship reversed his engine, full ahead port, full astern starboard, to swing the stern around to the U-boat.

The U-boat crash-dived. The destroyer dropped six depth charge. The U-boat turned to starboard, avoiding the charges.

*Highlander* and *Harvester* then sent the *Balzac* out of the way and began to hunt seriously. *Highlander* soon had a sound contact and dropped a flare to mark the spot. The two destroyers then began crisscrossing the area, and dropping depth charges. But the asdic again went out from concussion, and again the contact was lost.

The destroyers had, however, caused serious damage to the submarine. Fourteen depth charges came near, and they smashed the electrical system, stopped valves, broke the air pressure lines, started leaks, crushed the ballast tanks, smashed the depth gauge, and put the electric motors out of action so the boat could not escape underwater. The U-boat then fired two torpedoes, which were seen moving along by the two destroyers, and they made contact again by tracking them.

Five minutes after firing the torpedoes, the U-boat surfaced, moving at seven knots, stern down. She had obviously been damaged by some of the depth charges. The two destroyers then opened fire with their 4.7-inch guns and with machine guns. The U-boat's bow began to rise, went high in the air, and she began to sink, stern first. The *Harvester* stopped in the middle of a crowd of swimming men, and rescued twenty-nine survivors. The *Highlander* rescued four. Nine men were lost. Skipper Jenisch was among those saved, the first U-boat "star" captain to be captured.

When the Office of Naval Intelligence questioned these submariners, as a matter of routine, they learned a good deal about the German attitudes and plans. The crewmen of *U-32* shared Hitler's feeling that the British were already defeated but would not lie down and take their place in the New Order. They said that Germany was simply marking time, waiting for victory in the Battle of Britain, which must come soon.

As far as the air war was concerned, Britain was holding her own that autumn and inflicting serious damage on the Luftwaffe as it came to bomb. But the sea war offered greater danger. On December 1 Prime Minister Churchill called a special meeting of Admiralty officers, to discuss a tremendous undertaking, the laying of an enormous minefield from the seaward end of the North Channel, which gave access to the Mersey and Clyde rivers, to the hundred fathom line north-west of Ireland, three miles broad and sixty miles long from coastal waters to the ocean. The minefield would be laid deep, racing up to thirty-five feet from the surface, a depth of free water great enough to pass all ships, but which would entrap submarines. After a few submarines had been blown to smithereens, Churchill hoped, Admiral Doenitz would tire of the losing game and keep his submarines out of British waters.

"Here was the defensive in excelsis. Anyhow it was better than nothing. It was the last resort. Provisional approval and directions for detailed proposals to be presented were given on this night."

At the same time came a change of priorities. RAF coastal command would now come to dominate the outlets from the Mersey and Clyde rivers and around Northern Ireland. This was to become their primary task, and the bombing of Germany, which had heretofore been the number one assault task of the RAF, was to be given second place. Churchill was determined that the Battle of Britain would be won, and until it was won, it would take first place.

"All suitable machines and pilots and material must be concentrated on our counteroffensive, by fighters against enemy bombers, and surface craft, assisted by bombers, against the U-boats in these narrow vital waters."

At the end of November came a major change in the Battle of Britain. It had begun in July with the attacks on shipping and coastal targets. During the second week of August the full assault on the RAF fighters had begun. After that, the assault had moved progressively inland. Then the Germans had shifted their attack to London and had been resoundingly defeated on September 15. By October the Luftwaffe had stopped sending big bomber raids over in the daytime, only fighter bomber forays that were little more than nuisance value. The big attacks came at night, and although they did much damage, it was to civilian operations and not to the military.

During the battle, some serious differences about tactics began to develop within the British military establishment, and by November the discussions had created a great deal of tension in the RAF. Some squadron commanders held that it was better to mass together several squadrons and then attack the Germans, rather than trying to meet every bombing threat, as was being done. Douglas Bader, the commander of Squadron 242, was one such advocate, and he was supported by Air Marshal Leigh-Mallory, the commander of Fighter Group 12.

These views were brought to the attention of several members of Parliament, and the conduct of the RAF became a political issue of the day. On October 17 an important meeting was held, with the deputy chief of the air staff, Air Vice Marshal Sholto Douglas, in charge. Air Marshal Dowding was there, and Air Vice Marshal Park and several others, including Leigh-Mallory to press his views, and Squadron Commander Bader.

This meeting registered the discontent within the RAF over Air Marshal Dowding's policies (and his brusque manners). So what was called "the big wing controversy" played a major part in the next step in the Battle of Britain, the dismissal of Air Marshal Dowding at the end of November and the dismissal of Air Vice Marshal Park of Group 11 the following month. Sholto Douglas took Dowding's place, and Leigh-Mallory took Park's job.

By the end of the year, although the Battle of Britain still raged, such changes had come to the fighting force as to make it quite a different organization from the RAF that had faced the Luftwaffe in the summer of 1940.

# CHAPTER 16

# Southampton

The bombing of Coventry was the signal to the provinces that the holiday was over, and that any industrial area was likely to "get it" any night.

The civil defense officials and others in the Ministry of Home Security knew this, and a cogent report was drawn and circulated in November, dealing with the events of that night of Thursday, November 14.

What happened in Coventry confirmed the observation of what had happened in the East End of London. The officals could see that a more imaginative organization was needed to deal with the psychological and social effects of air attack. The physical apparatus, dealing with casualties, fires, gas, and debris, seemed quite adequate. But the method of dealing with the homeless was very bad, and no effort at all was made to help people who were not hurt, or homeless but totally disoriented by the bombings. In Coventry this element had numbered two hundred thousand people, and their attitudes had changed those of the town, and the areas around where they mingled with other people. The authorities found that this failure had an enormous although unmeasurable effect on morale and war production in the battered factories that remained.

If the authorities had simply devoted 5 percent of their effort to the problems of the apparently untouched, the effect

of the bombing would not have been nearly so bad as it was.
The following were needed:

Mobile canteens to appear almost immediately

A special propaganda flying squad to reassure the public

A loudspeaker van in the hands of skillful commentators
to reassure and give vital information

Special reserves of voluntary social workers

Special facilities for getting newspapers delivered and sold
in the streets

In fact, at Coventry these things had not been done by the
evening of Saturday, November 16, two days after the raid.
For two solid days the survivors had lived in a fog, not
knowing where to go, what to do.

The civil defense concept had been built around the rest
center as the source of all these amenities. But at Coventry,
of fifteen rest centers, thirteen were obliterated or damaged
in the raid and failed to function. Something better had to be
devised.

Another problem that spread a sort of panic among the
people was the almost total breakdown of transportation. The
debris had been cleared away from the streets very efficiently
by the first evening, and it was possible to drive everywhere
in the town. But no buses were running. Meanwhile many
trucks and buses that were used to transport policemen and
soldiers around the town were sitting idle. They could have
been lent to civil defense.

Another problem was not dealt with: the temporary repair
of houses. Most of the windows of Coventry had been blown
out, and the supply of repair materials was exhausted within
forty-eight hours. The authorities should have brought in
boarding to black out and close up houses and shops so they
could be used.

Another problem was the popular press, particularly of
London. What was needed were factual reports, emanating
from official sources, showing an appreciation of problems,
showing official action, and giving advice to the public about
what they could do for themselves or for others. What they

got was exaggerated accounts, what came to be called "courage stories," which were apparently designed by the editors to raise morale, but which actually created enormous suspicion of press reports among the public.

All this was known, but it was not accepted even in the ministry. When the report came out, it became the subject of squabbling in official circles, the national officials against the local, and consequently the bogging down of the whole.

Nor was the concept entirely new with the Coventry bombing. A number of cities smaller than London had been hit hard already. Southampton, with its Spitfire factory, had been a primary target in the beginning of the Luftwaffe assault on the British fighters. The first air raid at Southampton had come on June 19, 1940, and the city had been alerted for raids sixteen hundred times since then until the middle of November. Bristol, too, had been a target, and so had several other cities that boasted fighter production facilities.

Most of the attacks had been made in daylight, by a handful of planes, and they had purposefully sought first the docks, in that summer campaign ordained by Hitler against shipping and docks as a preliminary to the Battle of Britain and the invasion, and the Supermarine factory and the docks. The Luftwaffe had accomplished its mission with the Supermarine factory and in October destroyed production there, although by that time Spitfire production did not fail, because it had been dispersed to thirty-five smaller units. Southampton was then a city of about 180,000 people, and until the middle of November 1940, even though the aircraft factory had been bombed and some bombs had fallen around the city, it had been accepted that the real target was aircraft, not people. But on the night of Sunday, November 17, all this changed. It was just three days after the devastation of Coventry. The Coventry report was out, but nothing was being done about it.

A hundred fifty-nine German bombers came over, dropping two hundred tons of high explosives and nearly five hundred incendiary canisters.

The second raid in the new series came six nights later, on November 23, when 121 bombers brought 150 tons of high explosive and again nearly five hundred canisters of incendiaries.

The third raid was on the night of November 30 and extended into the following morning, when the Germans bombed with 251 planes, bringing three hundred tons of high explosive and nearly twelve hundred canisters of incendiaries.

At the end of this treatment, Southampton lay in ruins. An official report had this to say:

> The damage to domestic and business dwellings is, so far as we can judge, more severe than at any other place yet studied.
>
> The raids were violent for nights in succession.
>
> The topographical factor is also important in interpreting the Southampton experience. Around the center of the city is an unusually wide area of park, lawn and open space; there is not the densely clustered core of a city such as existed in Coventry and was totally ruined there. In Southampton, the equivalent area is the main street, running through the Bargate. This has been shattered from end to end.
>
> Finally, the population of Southampton is to a high extent genuinely resident and locally interested. Southampton has deeper social roots than Coventry or Stepney. There is a certain tradition of local toughness, partly associated with the docks and the sea.

The people had to be tough to contemplate the damage done by the Luftwaffe to their city.

The main shopping area had been virtually gutted. Very few major stores were open. A large part of the business area was almost destroyed; only two of the main banks were functioning.

Most of the city's cinemas, halls, and churches had suffered severe damage, particularly from the fire bombing, and the crowded district where the shopkeepers and workingmen lived east of the town center had been hard hit. Several acres had been reduced to pure rubble.

The factory areas were heavily bombed, the Pirelli Cable Works was a tangled ruin, and the Ranks Flour Mill storage tower was half sheared away. The Southampton docks were bombed heavily, and most of the dock wharves and sheds were tangled masses of chaos.

Other parts of the town were bombed; a majority of houses probably sustained some damage, but the area around the ferries was not so badly hit as the rest.

The more expensive residential area on the west side of Southampton in the main got off very lightly.

A reporter went to the hotel on the third night, after two nights of bombing. He found a battery set working the radio in the lounge because there was no electricity, and all the guests around to catch the nine o'clock news on the BBC.

In the aftermath of the raids, the character of the town changed. An investigator coming into town at the docks on the evening of December 2 found the town apparently dead, with no cars moving and very few people. But what had happened was that the people who came in to work had gone out again. An estimated 30 percent of the population fled outright. Another third became floaters, who came in the morning and left in the evenings. The towns around and the villages were full to overflowing.

The civil government virtually collapsed. The chief constable walking on the street in the early hours of the morning after the December 1 raid was hit by a car and injured, and put out of action. The mayor and his defense committee seemed unable to cope, and the Ministry of Home Security stepped in and began to make some order out of the mess. The recovery of the city was hampered by the blowing of the main switchboards of the telephone system in the post office on November 30, and the inability of the *Southern Evening Echo* to publish for several days. The main post office at the civic center was not badly damaged, but closed, and no one knew where to go to post letters or to get information.

So the experience at Coventry had not done any good, although all the recommendations had been made, and had they been followed in Southampton, they would have spared the people much suffering and would have brought order back to the city.

Everything was chaos until Monday afternoon, December

2, when a van began to move around the city with a loud-speaker repeating one message:

"The pipe water is undrinkable. REPEAT. The pipe water is undrinkable."

The van moved quickly and the loudspeaker in the front pointed straight ahead, so that many people did not make out the message even though they heard it. The van soon broke down and the confusion reigned supreme once more.

Most of the water mains had been cut off. Gas and light were off in most of the city. So if you were to boil your water, people asked, how do you boil it?

If one could find an offical and ask about the factories, he would say:

"Go to one of the labor exchanges and get that information."

But the labor exchanges had set up in obscure places and were impossible for people to find. Most administrative buildings were either gutted or disarranged. The army recruiting office was burned out, with no word about where the soldiers could be found. The pensions department was deserted.

The municipal health department office had a notice on the door, scrawled by hand:

NO ENTRY. DANGEROUS.

The would-be helpers who came down from London to investigate for the Home Office found that pensioners and the old did not know where to go or what to do. The pregnant could not find a doctor or a nurse. The ill could not find treatment. People who wanted to evacuate could not get the forms or information.

The military came in to help and managed to make matters worse by taking over the best remaining office space. They knew nothing about local conditions, but they spoke with the voice of authority.

When the *Echo* reappeared—four pages instead of the usual twenty—it contained no helpful announcements from authority. The big story was a warning to local business from the Home Office not to collect information about air raid damage, because this would make them liable for legal proceedings.

And how was one to escape the town if one decided to go? There were no announcements, buses did not run on schedule or on their usual routes, and no one came forth with information. The civic center possessed a public notice board, but nothing went up on it until December 4. The notice, when it finally went up, was not much help.

PEOPLE OF SOUTHAMPTON

Although the town has been severely damaged it has not suffered any permanent injury. Some of the public services such as gas and water are temporarily interrupted, but the necessary repairs will be quickly carried out and the services will be operating again in a few days' time.

The principal works and factories are continuing to operate and they will be able to employ all or the majority of their ordinary staff. Everybody should get in touch with his employer or the nearest Labor Exchange in order to resume his work.

Temporary transport arrangements will be made in order that people may get to work without difficulty.

The Battle of Britain must go on. All Southampton must continue to play its vital part.

Harold B. Butler
Regional Commissioner

H. Lewis
Mayor of Southampton

It was a week before the situation at the civic center had improved any.

The big problem was to get something to eat. Bread was in short supply, but all rationed commodities were hard to find. Some shops were bombed out, but many were just closed. Very few cafés and restaurants were open. There was no communal feeding at first.

It was December 4 before things began to happen to alleviate the food problems. St. Michael's Church Hall opened a canteen. It turned out to be operated by the Christian Scientists, not Church of England. Two weeks later this was still the leading public center for food in the town, and there was only one other.

The *Echo* by this time was advertising Christmas turkeys, Christmas wines and spirits.

And who could buy these?

Only the rich who had connections to find them.

Several mobile canteens arrived and set up. One went into the Polygon Hotel, which had become police headquarters, and most of its cups of tea went to the police, who had their own canteen inside. Another seemed to cater only to men in uniform. None of them sought out the townspeople.

The pubs went back into action of a sort. Some served beer only in daylight hours. By December 2 cigarettes were unobtainable, and it was weeks before the supplies caught up.

For some reason, King George VI arrived on December 5 and outside the civic center inspected a parade of civil defense workers, police and firemen, and members of the gas, water, and electic departments.

This was supposed to be a morale-building activity for Southampton and the nation. The national press and radio carried the story, but no loudspeaker van announced the king's coming. The party passed almost unnoticed.

When they read about the king's visit in the newspapers, people were not much impressed. It was all right to have the king come, some said, but they would rather have a new house. Notices began to go up listing the known dead and injured, with addresses. Some firms put up notices for their staffs. There were no notices from the Ministry of Information, although some notices were posted outside empty shops telling people to go to the civic center for information about recreation, evacuation, transportation, and air raid precaution. But at the civic center the people on duty were so busy, they had no time to answer general inquiries.

What happened to the churches? Did they pitch in to succor the people?

No churchmen appeared to perform, nor did any of the voluntary organizations like the Salvation Army. One priest said it was useless to be concerned, because the Southampton people were an irreligious lot who did not go to church. It was true, as they claimed that their churches had been bombed out. But the clergymen were mostly intact, and not visible. The fact was that the clergy had turned away from the people, and the people had turned away from the clergy.

One Anglican warden said that bombing had put a stop to churchgoing. The people weren't very religious anyhow, he admitted, but now they didn't come to church at all. They just disappeared from the town.

A Catholic priest whose church had been bombed said he did not believe the people had any desire for God. There were churches quite near that they could attend, but the Southampton people were not visible there.

Southampton had boasted good air raid facilities—at least as good as any of the other coastal cities. They were better than the Coventry shelters by far. And they stood up well. But the people did not really believe in them. On the following Saturday, December 7, when the air raid warnings sounded, only three shelters were full; the rest had only a third as many people as they could hold, and one contained one single civil defense official.

That weekend only five bombs fell in the whole area, and these were jettisoned from aircraft in trouble. In all the rest of December, only one person was killed and one house destroyed, and the same story was repeated in January 1941.

The last bombing of the winter came to Southampton on Sunday, January 9. The bombs were scattered widely; they destroyed seven houses and damaged a hundred, killing one person and injuring three. After that, nothing more as the weeks went by. The bombers went elsewhere; again the Germans felt that they had "finished" Southampton. London was bombed more, and several other cities were heavily bombed.

Southampton did not "recover" from the bombings, in the usual sense. Many of the people who had left the town did not come back. Those who had moved to surrounding towns and villages and "trekked" into Southampton, to work or to shop, continued to do so instead of coming back to live. Life assumed a different pattern.

Officials from London who came to Southampton to survey

the scene found that morale here had distinctly deteriorated following the heavy bombing. The reason was the shortage of people, so many did not come back, and the failure of the authorities to rally the people. The government and social organizations continued in their lethargy.

The public utilities still were not put right, and thousands of houses had broken windows and leaky roofs, which made them unpleasant to live in even if they were livable. Thus in the wintry weather, even more people deserted their homes and went elsewhere. The authorities had surveyed seven houses just after the first bombings to see what people were eating, and what supplies they had. They came back two weeks later and found that six of the seven houses were now vacant.

The reason was not food shortage. By mid-January the food situation had improved greatly. The real shortage was candles, which remained the principal source of lighting.

The reason was not fear, either. The people seemed to sense after the January raid that the Germans had turned elsewhere.

A sort of lasting shock seemed to have much to do with the attitude of the people. They continued to talk about the raids until outside observers characterized this behavior as a neurosis. The authorities did nothing to change the situation, no campaign of local pride, nothing.

One trouble in Southampton was that a month after the bombing, there was virtually nothing to do with leisure time; only one pub had a pianist and a singer. The authorities might have learned something had they gone there, because this pub did twice as much business as any other, and the talk inside was cheerful and laughing. The other pubs were somber, and most of them were virtually empty.

The strongest feeling expressed in Southampton was that things would never be the same again.

# CHAPTER 17

# *Defeat Into Victory*

By December 1940 the tempo of bombing in London had settled down. The city was being hit somewhere every night, but a sameness had set in that made it difficult for observers—particularly journalists—to find anything new to write or talk about. Edward R. Murrow, in his reports for CBS, was reduced to telling stories such as the one about the journalist in a small village who was mistaken for a German spy, and nearly arrested in the pub, until the people realized that his "*Ja*" was really "Yeah" and that the code words he seemed to be writing in his notebook were nothing but shorthand notes.

The reporters complained about censorship, but the fact was that they were free—as was the general public—to express any opinions they wished, and they were getting information about the successes and failures in the Battle of Britain, from the ominous and growing figures of monthly shipping losses, to the heartening figures on aircraft production, which was higher in October than in September and would continue to grow, despite the continuing air battle and bombing.

Life somehow was a little easier in London that winter but the Germans bombed Southampton and Portsmouth. Portsmouth then was a city of about 250,000 people, about twice the population of Southampton. Seventy-four bombers came over that December night. Then came a lull, and then the Germans returned again on January 10, 1941.

The damage, most of it done in the January raid, included the almost complete destruction of one of the city's main shopping centers and the gutting by high explosive and fire of the civic center.

Again, the advice tendered in the Home Ministry about Coventry was not followed here, and the result was a population seriously shaken by the raids. Further, there was deep resentment of officialdom by the poor, who accused the well-to-do of "trekking"—coming to the city by day to work and then leaving in the evening for the safety of southeast Hampshire and Sussex. Counts of private cars showed that 38 percent of the cars had three or sometimes four passengers, 55 percent had two, and 7 percent had only a single driver.

Portsmouth people were putting a great strain on the surrounding countryside, in a half circle fifteen miles back from the coast. It was charged that they were clogging the roads, filling up the hotels and snapping up the housing, and taking over the pubs and restaurants that belonged to the local people, while back in Portsmouth, the streets and most of the pubs were empty after dusk. The resentments grew deep. And, it was soon learned, those abandoning the city by night were not just the "toffs," but the working-class people as well. An official study showed that 50 to 60 percent of the people in densely populated sectors of the city had abandoned Portsmouth, at least during the nighttime hours.

In Portsmouth, as in Southampton, the authorities distanced themselves from the people. After the burn-out of the civic center, the town clerk moved his office to a hotel on the waterfront, out of touch with virtually everything and everybody. Police headquarters moved to a college some distance from the city center. The public assistance office was miles away in another building, and the public health offices were in a fourth location.

The churches again did not seem to be on the same side as the people. All vestiges of the burned-out churches seemed to vanish; there was no sign of the churchmen in the affairs of the community. It was as if they had never been, except for one occasion.

On January 17, after the second big raid, Portsmouth held a mass burial. It was a grand affair, attended by the lord mayor with his gold chain and medals, the town clerk, the Anglican bishop and the Catholic bishop in full regalia, the lesser clergy in their round collars, city councillors, and naval and army officers. The procession was led by a naval commander, and it crossed the city from Alexandra Park to Kingston Cemetery, the main procession led by the Royal Marine Band, followed by an undertaker in a top hat, followed by twelve Daimler and Rolls-Royce hearses with drivers in top hats, the hearses carrying coffins draped with the British Union Jack flag. Soldiers and sailors and marines walked alongside, as pallbearers, all in slow march, with the muffled drums and muted trombones setting cadence.

The police were out to control the spectators who lined the route to the grave. It was a hundred feet long, lined with Union Jacks; at one end stood fifty mourners, at the other fifty clergymen, led by the bishops.

The effect of this show seemed to be to depress most of the people of Portsmouth, and set back the city's recovery by several weeks. In this, the Germans scored a significant victory, for their whole program of bombing the lesser cities was designed for this purpose, as much to wreck British morale as to harass industrial targets. As Blitz historian Tom Harrisson put it: "The idea was still to dislocate the whole area, by shattering social and domestic patterns at least as much as anything directly industrial or military; in the ports, naval and dock personnel supplied an added attraction."

The fact was that Coventry, Southampton, and Portsmouth represented Luftwaffe victory in a sense, but it was a frustrated victory, because although the social and community lives of these cities and towns was destroyed, the workmen continued to report to their factories and they continued to maintain the British war machine.

As for Southampton, in the last part of January that town began to show new signs of life, mostly through the efforts of private enterprise. The city officials could not seem to get organized and provide the public with much information about anything, but the Southampton chamber of commerce could. That month the chamber produced a twenty-four-page booklet, "The Emergency Business Directory," which indicated which firms were still doing business in the community and what they did. It sold for two pence per copy. An organization called the Fairway Corner Fire Party set up shop to clean up the city, and asked for donations of ten shillings for a "fighting fund." They enlisted volunteers to provide fire protection and to meet much less obvious needs, such as building cleanup.

Public facilities began to come to life in Southampton, too, and by the end of February, transport and telephone systems were slowly being restored. But many of the public telephone boxes did not work, and the public transportation facilities closed down around dark. Taxis were available, but not after 6:00 P.M., which meant approaching darkness and possible air raid. Night life was still dead because of the fear of the bombers. Cinemas all closed by 8:00 P.M., and the Grand Theater did not open at all. Pubs did good business, but they did not open their lounge bars, which catered to ladies, except on weekends. Trekking and evacuation were still the hallmarks of the community, busy by day, deserted by night and on weekends. But Banister Dance Hall, a low and bawdy establishment that catered to drunken servicemen, was open every weeknight from 7:00 to 10:00 P.M. in a private house near the Sportsdrome. Young girls and servicemen thronged there to meet, sit at tables, dance, and drink. At least it was social life of a sort.

March 1, a Saturday, saw the first air raid in weeks. There had been a number of alerts, but no bombs had fallen on Southampton. Many people had stopped carrying their gas masks, a sure sign of insouciance. When the warnings came, no one went to the shelters. But the Saturday warning was followed by the appearance of misty contrails high in the sky and puffs of smoke from antiaircraft guns, so the onlookers below began to decide that something might be about to happen that they would not enjoy. They began to head for the shelters. The all clear sounded and the people emerged from the shelters. That afternoon the incidence of gas mask carrying doubled.

March moved along. Recovery of small businesses and private facilities picked up. Commercial restaurants opened and stayed open, giving people a real choice, but mostly for lunch. The evening was still too much of an uncertain quantity. The Tolia offered curried turkey; the Michel put out a four-course luncheon, of soup, pasta, veal, and bacon, and a dessert. At the more expensive end of town, the Dolphin Hotel and Gatti's served more expensive food.

The talk among citizens veered away from the bombings, but citizens always liked to tell strangers their old stories, and sometimes to conduct them on tours of the bombing. "That was the library, before the bomb hit . . . That was the furrier's . . . That was Boot's, the chemist . . ."

Taxes went up and people began to complain, a very healthy sign. But many businesses could not reopen, because they could not get supplies, or they did not trust the future. One chemist's shop posted a list of the items it did not have, which seemed to be more than what it did have: no lipsticks, soap, razor blades, or shaving cream.

Although many people still trekked and many townspeople still were on the vanished list, new people began to move into Southampton, declaring that they were coming because they believed it was safe, now that the bombing had passed by. They were not quite right. Southampton was bombed again on March 11, but it was a light raid; only seventy bombs fell, and the damage was not very great. From this time on, although the town was bombed again in 1942 and 1943, the damage was really insignificant. Southampton was a safe place to be if you were going to be in England, after the spring of 1941.

Portsmouth was not so fortunate. It was raided again on April 17 by 249 bombers, and on April 27 by 38 bombers, which dropped bombs and land mines that created a new sort of problem. Still the authorities seemed to be numb to the problems of the people. It was not until the middle of May that they put on their thinking caps. The lord mayor that day reported to the council that he had seen the regional commissioner and told him that something had to be done to evacuate women and children from the city, because 75 percent of the people he had talked to wanted to get out. The regional commissioner took the matter up with the Ministry of Health, which opposed such evacuation. Faced with a growing spirit of rebellion in Portsmouth, the ministry did agree to "make a study," and a distinguished retired admiral was chosen to make it. But the study languished, and the people and city council became impatient and angry. Months had gone by and the women and children were still subject to bombing. In fact, many people had already left.

The people who remained were nervous from the strain. Some of them had money problems; everyone had trouble with adjusting to the rationing. Gas pressures rose and fell, making cooking difficult, and the houses suffered broken windows and other shock damage.

April was also the month in which Bristol had its last big raid by the Luftwaffe. The city had been hit six times since November 24, 1940, the last time on April 11, 1941. Plymouth was raided in November, but then left alone until spring, when it received seven big raids. One of them came on March 20. That day King George VI and the queen had come down from London to take tea with Lady Astor. They toured the town and said all the proper things and then went back to London at 6:00 P.M. That night and the next, Plymouth had its heaviest raids, involving 293 planes dropping 346 tons of bombs.

These raids and the four April raids on Plymouth were the result of discussions in Germany between the Luftwaffe and Admiral Doenitz's U-boat corps. In twelve weeks, between mid-February and mid-May, thirty-nine raids were directed against the western and southwestern ports, in Germany's effort to cut the British lifeline that brought supplies in from the west. Prime Minister Churchill was well aware of what the Germans were doing, and more than a little worried by it.

At the end of 1940, as the Blitz bombing continued and the German submarine menace became much worse, Churchill had written a long letter to President Roosevelt calling for help in what he saw as the mutual problem of self-preservation. (''We must do our best to prevent the German domination of Europe, spreading into Africa and into Southern Asia.'') He did not want American troops, Churchill said, but he did need help. The danger of Britain being destroyed or invaded had receded that fall, but an equally deadly danger had arisen: the German campaign of attrition on the sea and in the air. The worst problem was the effectiveness of U-boat activity and bombing against British shipping. In 1941 the crisis would be forced on Britain by the Germans: could the

British maintain their lifeline to the west, on which the whole war effort depended?

British shipping losses were frightening in this sixteenth month of the war. In the week ending November 4, ship losses had reached a total of 420,000 tons. Britain had to import forty-three million tons, but the rate of importation had fallen to thirty-eight million tons. At this rate of losses, Britain would soon be finished. The big problem was that Britain was surrounded by enemies, who were basing their submarines and aircraft in France. They also had the surface raiders to contend with in this Battle of Britain.

So what did Britain want from America?

1. Reassertion of the doctrine of freedom of the seas
2. American escorts to protect American shipping to Britain
3. American warships, particularly destroyers
4. Help in dealing with Eire, for bases
5. Three million more tons of ships per year
6. Two thousand military aircraft per month
7. Munitions and weapons for ten divisions
8. Credit or grants to pay for supplies produced in America

Churchill's letter was sent to President Roosevelt, and it became the basis for the president's decision to undertake the Lend-Lease program of assistance to Britain.

So Lend-Lease came into being in February 1941, and with it a much greater and growing American commitment to the British in the war.

Since September 1940, the Germans had been conducting unrestricted submarine warfare in the Atlantic—another part of the Battle of Britain. The seriousness of it was indicated by the story of Convoy HX112, which consisted of forty-one freighters and tankers escorted by five destroyers and two corvettes. Between March 16 and March 18 this convoy lost five ships, but at the same time, five U-boats were sunk. The Germans responded by moving the center of their U-boat activity westward to the point where the Canadian escorts left the convoys, and before the British joined up to take over. The idea was to catch the convoys without escorts. The plan worked on the night of April 3, when Convoy SC26 was caught in the open, and ten of the twenty-two ships were sunk in that one night, at a cost of two U-boats.

The first American involvement in the battle occurred on April 10, when the U.S. destroyer *Niblack* picked up three boatloads of survivors from a torpedoed Netherlands freighter. When they were moving away, the destroyer's sound operator picked up a submarine, and the destroyer division commander ordered the *Niblack* to attack. The destroyer dropped depth charges, and the submarine moved away from the area.

The intensive bombings were having a bad effect on the morale of the politicians in Britain. Herbert Morrison, the minister of home security, was one of the ones to panic, and kept telling anyone who would listen that the morale of the coastal towns, like Plymouth, was shot to pieces. But Prime Minister Churchill had a different view, which he wanted to promulgate. At four o'clock on the afternoon of May 2, the prime minister arrived at Plymouth for a morale-building tour. By that time thousands of the daily trekkers were on their way to their digs, wherever they were, and only a small percentage of the town's official population remained to have a look at him. About thirty-five hundred people lined the streets as the car came down, with loudspeaker vans ahead, announcing his coming. He was perched on the back of the open car seat, with Mrs. Churchill at his side and Lady Astor, who was mayoress of Plymouth and a member of Parliament. People cheered him as he came, and he gave the Churchillian grin and the V-for-victory sign. The car stopped twice, once outside the guild hall. Those who got close were very well impressed; the prime minister exuded an air of vitality and confidence that did them good to see. He was also moved by deep emotion. "God bless you all," he said, and "Well done, Plymouth"—both statements with tears in his eyes.

"Good old Winnie," shouted the crowd. And the prime minister smiled and the car moved away.

# CHAPTER 18

# *The Battle Continued*

All through the last of 1940 and well into 1941 the bombing of London continued, but more attention was given to the industrial cities of northern England. Hitler's mind had switched to his plans for the invasion of Russia, but he had not wavered, he still intended to invade England as soon as possible unless the British gave up and opted out of the war.

The twin cities of Liverpool and Birkenhead on the Mersey River had been major targets for the Luftwaffe since the beginning of the battle, although the major effort was to come late in the year and in the winter and spring of 1941. Four night raids in August 1940 sent a total of 448 bombers over these two cities. To be sure, the raids did not match the London raids in intensity, but they were serious enough, against cities totalling 1.3 million people that were centers of shipping and manufacturing.

The area, generally called Merseyside, was the major British port for the Atlantic and the beginning of the sea lane to North America. Thus it received major attention from the Luftwaffe, as the sea lanes outside received from the U-boat corps. Ultimately there would be sixteen major attacks, eight of them ranked as heavy.

After those first four days in August, the Germans seemed to forget about Merseyside, but then on the night of November 28, 1940, the Luftwaffe was back with 324 planes.

In Liverpool the sirens began to sound at seven-thirty that night. It was the first time in four days that the sirens had wailed. The previous nights the raids had not materialized here, the aircraft were heading elsewhere. No one was really prepared for the raid. Slowly people began to seek shelter, either in the Anmerson portable shelters in their backyards, or in the public shelters in basements and large buildings.

For the first two hours no one noticed much except the sound of antiaircraft gunfire, the noise of airplane engines, and the sound of the concussion of bombs. The area seemed to quiet down, although there was no all clear sounded, so many people went out of the shelters. But then the guns started all over again as a new wave of attackers came in. This time they were using incendiaries, and a number of houses went up in smoke.

The next raid on Merseyside came just before Christmas 1940. Two night raids, two nights of terror, with high explosive and incendiaries all around. But the people of Merseyside neither panicked nor became obsessed with the air raids as had happened in the port cities of the south. Liverpudlians were cheerful through it all, walking along, singing and whistling in the streets.

> "Bless 'em all, bless 'em all,
> The long, and the short, and the tall . . ."

Unlike Coventry, unlike Southampton, unlike Plymouth, city life and shopping continued, almost unchanged. There was plenty of transportation at night, plenty of taxicabs, even during air raids. Restaurants were open and serving meals until 9:00 P.M. The pubs were open and crowded with people until closing time. A number of cinemas and theaters were open at night, playing to moderately full houses. Matinee performances were always crowded. The dance halls were full of laughing people.

The incidence of gas mask carrying—always a sign of anxiety—was very low. Children and women were very conspicuous by their continued presence. Only a few of those eligible for evacuation had chosen to leave.

The whole atmosphere was jolly, almost holidayesque in

nature. In Liverpool on the nights between Christmas and New Year, five or six hundred people could be found in a central dance hall, while enemy planes were overhead.

The people of Liverpool laughed their way through the Blitz, more or less. One of their major preoccupations was gibing at the city government. They told how the town clerk ran the government, for he also had the titles of clerk of the rating authority (Taxes), clerk of education, clerk of old age pensions, clerk of public assistance, clerk of licenses, commissioner of income tax, clerk to the Mersey Tunnel Authority, food controller, light and fuel overseer, and coordinator of all air raid precautions. He was the Lord Pooh-Bah over everything and everybody.

January and February were times of quiet on Merseyside, with no big attacks. Had it not been for news of continued raids on London and raids on other cities, one might have thought that the Battle of Britain was over. But there was always sobering news these days from the docksides, when the sailors came in from their convoys and told about the U-boat wolf packs out there, hunting for their prey.

Then in March came two raids, almost two hundred planes per night, and in April two raids, and in May five raids. And at the end of it, it was apparent that the Germans had accomplished one of the things they set out to do, at least in the Merseyside area. The people of Liverpool, just weeks before so confident and uncaring, had been turned by the intensity of these raids. The public air raid shelters were cold and inhospitable, and many people would not go to them. The rest centers, where meals and sleeping accommodations were supposed to be provided, were regarded as totally inadequate, even "hopeless." Emergency feeding arrangements in the city had almost collapsed. Mobile canteens seemed always to be in the wrong place at the wrong time or nowhere at all. No hot food was available to most city residents for days at a time. The night spots closed, the dance halls were empty; the pubs that did stay open ran out of beer. Cigarettes were unobtainable; public transportation was in chaos, and private taxis were almost impossible to find. As one citizen put it, "There was no more power or drive left in Liverpool."

As elsewhere, the authorities had deserted the people, and clung to their high posts and talked only to themselves. A sense of defeat hovered over the city, where information about almost anything was impossible to obtain.

The failure of the authorities to issue information bulletins led to the race of rumors around Liverpool. After the last big raid of May 7, the police temporarily closed the city's center to cars and people without special business, so they could clean up the debris. But they did not tell anyone this, and they sought the assistance of army personnel to police the blocked points. So the rumor began that Liverpool had been put under martial law, and soon the story was in London, and was being repeated by members of Parliament, otherwise responsible newspaper editors, civil servants, and clerics. Soon the story was all over England and survived. As of the end of the war, there were still people who believed that martial law had been placed over Liverpool, because the people had become rebellious and intractable.

The winter of 1941 was called "the happy time" by the German U-boat captains. They had the British naval codes, which helped them by indicating the sailing and arrival of convoys. These were signal months in the Battle of the Atlantic, which was a part of the Battle of Britain, and here Prime Minister Churchill, who had been growingly concerned about the German successes, found considerable cause for concern. The U-boats had perfected the wolf pack technique, which was very effective against convoys. The wolf packs presented two new problems to the British defenders:

1. How to defend convoys against the high-speed night attack in which only destroyers could move fast enough to deal with the U-boats?

Asdic was of no use at all against a fast-moving U-boat on the surface. Part of the solution lay in the increase of the number of destroyers in the convoy screen, very difficult because there were not enough destroyers to go around.

Another part of the solution lay in the improvement of radar, and this offered a quicker and more immediately hopeful approach. But for the moment, the losses were high and would continue to be high for a while.

2. The second problem was how to exploit the very definite

vulnerabilty of a surfaced U-boat, which was a relatively big and easily damaged target. What was needed was a better air weapon, better depth bombs, better delivered by more aircraft. But although the aircraft were in "the pipeline," it would be another two years before sufficient numbers of such aircraft as the B-24 Liberator bomber, ideal for long-range antisubmarine work, would be available.

Still, the men who manned the small ships that fought the U-boats had developed some new techniques and a great deal of skill, which began to show themselves.

The end of 1941 found the German effort in the sea Battle of Britain at a low ebb, after a fierce attack period. Earlier in December Captain Mergerson in *U-101* had found Convoy HX90, and Admiral Doenitz had assembled a wolf pack. The pack took ten ships from HX90 and damaged one other, and the Luftwaffe sank one. But in this effort the U-boats expended all their torpedoes and had to return to their bases to rearm.

Thus at Christmastime 1940, only one U-boat was at sea, Lieutenant Salman's *U-52*. This was the weakness of Admiral Doenitz's operation, through no fault of his own. He had repeatedly asked, before the war, for increased U-boat production, but Hitler always had some other way to spend the money, and now that Doenitz had the best weapon so far devised against the British, he did not have the U-boats to employ it properly.

The year came in like a lion in the eastern Atlantic, with storm following storm, weather that was hard on U-boat crews but ideal for U-boat attacks on convoys. The U-boats that went out to fight the Battle of Britain were beset by storms and fog. Also, with the increased awareness of the British War Cabinet of the U-boat danger as more significant in the long run than the danger from bombing, the British Admiralty had begun to route convoys in new ways, to confuse the U-boats. The most significant development in this effort was radio direction finding. Bearings were taken on every U-boat's radio transmission, and these were triangulated. Thus the Royal Navy was able to keep fairly good track of the U-boats at sea. The areas in which they operated were avoided like the plague.

Because of the knowledge gained from British and French documents captured in the fall of France, the German knew how much value the British put on their radio intelligence, although they did not know, because the British had not told the French, that the British had one of the German special coding machines called Ultra, and thus could decode many messages that concerned U-boat operations.

Ideally, then, U-boats should maintain complete radio silence. But the rub was that the sighting reports of U-boats were the major source of Admiral Doenitz's intelligence, because while the Germans had captured British codes early in the war, some of the codes had now been changed. What was really wanted was cooperation with an air force. Here the difficulty stemmed from Reichsmarschal Goering's almost absolute control of German air forces. The navy had an air wing, but it consisted mostly of aircraft carried by ships and flown off from them. The Luftwaffe controlled the land-based air, and although Goering promised cooperation and delivered some, he was extremely stingy in the use of his air squadrons for reconnaissance work that would benefit the navy.

At one stage all the U-boats west of 145 degrees west longitude were ordered to make daily reports on sightings and weather to the U-boat arm, but this was stopped when it was discovered that the British were using the transmissions to reroute their convoys.

Therefore, for the time being at least, Doenitz had to relinquish his iron control, send his boats into the operations areas assigned them, and hope for the best results.

As far as reconnaissance was concerned, the Luftwaffe that summer and early fall had made available an average of only four planes a day. Air Group 40 allocated a single Focke Wulff 200 bomber every day without fail to the U-boat arm. Other groups were supposed to do the same, but always it was "due to technical defects, there are no planes." Doenitz became so disgusted, he began to refer to the Luftwaffe as "eagles without wings."

The situation became so difficult that in December, Doenitz prepared a memo for Admiral Raeder. The admiral gave his full support to the U-boat approach to the problem, and arranged a meeting between Doenitz and General Jodl, chief of operations for OKW, Hitler's supreme command of all the armed forces.

They met on January 2, 1941, and Admiral Doenitz asked for at least twelve long-range reconnaissance planes at all times. Jodl listened but did not comment.

Then Hitler took a hand, prodded by Admiral Raeder. He ordered that Air Group 40 be placed under the operational control of the U-boat command. Reichsmarschal Goering did not like this, but there was nothing he could do about it. Hitler was determined to win the Battle of Britain. No one could gainsay him.

The FW-200s were the only German aircraft with long enough range to reach twenty degrees west longitude. It seemed as though Doenitz had won his battle with the air force when operations began in mid-January. But the first convoy sighting report led to nothing. The Focke Wulffs found the convoy, but there were no submarines near. When they came back the next day, the convoy had changed course and speed and they could not relocate it.

But on February 9 the *U-37* sighted a convoy bound for Gibraltar, and Air Group 40 was alerted. Five Focke Wulffs attacked the convoy and sank several ships. The *U-37* continued to shadow the convoy, and the cruiser *Admiral Hipper*, which was out on raiding, found the convoy on February 12, and sank more ships. This was the first instance of cooperation—and successful cooperation—of air and sea and undersea units in the Battle of Britain.

Goering, who was furious with Admiral Doenitz for taking even one of his aircraft, managed to persuade Hitler that it was very bad for Luftwaffe morale to have air force units under navy control, so Hitler gave control of the Focke Wulff group back to Goering, on the proviso that he would cooperate with Doenitz.

Goering appointed Lieutenant Colonel Harlinghausen to run the air group, as Atlantic commander, and Harlinghausen took up residence near Lorient. He was an old navy pilot who understood the needs of the U-boats, and he established good relations with Doenitz. But he did not have enough aircraft; Goering saw to that. Never were more than two FWs available for work over the North Channel. Still, on February 23 an

FW-200 led the *U-73* to convoy OB288, and *U-73* brought four other U-boats in for a wolf pack attack at night, which sank nine ships.

But the problem was that the Luftwaffe pilots were not skilled at navigation and many of their sighting reports were inaccurate. The U-boats were doing better with their own kind. Lieutenant Topp in *U-552* found Convoy OB289; two more boats were called, and they sank three ships and damaged one. OB290 went out, through North Channel, and was sighted by Prien in *U-47*. He called back; six FW-200s arrived and sank nine ships. Prien also sank several ships and damaged some more.

The result of the new cooperation was the shooting up of British shipping losses, back near the three-hundred-thousand-ton mark for the month of February.

But at U-boat headquarters, Lieutenant Oehrn, the director of operations, made a study of the air-sea cooperative effort. He noted that the Luftwaffe often could not find a convoy on the second day and that if it did find the convoy, then its reports to the U-boat service might be in error by as much as seventy miles. Since U-boats made less than twenty-five knots on the surface at high speed, such a discrepancy made it very unlikely that convoys would ever be found. So Oehrn concluded reluctantly that the Luftwaffe was too ill trained in navigation and the Luftwaffe aircraft did not have sufficient range (there were no heavy bombers) to make the air reconnaissance of much use to the submarines. When the Luftwaffe got reports from the U-boats they were accurate as to location, but when the U-boats got reports from the air force, they were usually inaccurate and wasted much of the time of the U-boats.

So Doenitz decided that it was not as useful as it should be to rely on Luftwaffe sighting reports, and the U-boats began to work alone once more.

Dr. Goebbels's propaganda ministry was concentrating on the successes of the U-boats this winter, perhaps to mask the failure of the Luftwaffe to force Britain to surrender. The names of Prien, Schepke, Kretschmer, Schultze, Schuhart, Rollmann, and Lemp became household words in Germany;

these were the heroes who had each sunk more than one-hundred-thousand tons of enemy shipping.

In February 1941 three of Doenitz's most successful captains were back on duty in the Atlantic after leave and work on their boats. Schepke in the *U-100* sailed from Germany, across the North Sea and around the north of Scotland. Kretschmer's *U-99* left Lorient, and on February 20 Prien's *U-47* also left Lorient.

Prien was the first to find a convoy, and he began to shadow one convoy, and he sent a number of reports, and said he had sunk twenty-two-thousand tons of shipping. By the end of the month he had sunk five ships. But he had become extremely wary of using the radio, and Doenitz did not have any messages at all from *U-47* for the rest of that month, because he had ordered the spring U-boat offensive to begin on March 1.

Erich Topp in *U-552* was the one to find the first convoy of the month, HX109 bound east to England with war supplies. Topp reported in, and Doenitz moved four U-boats to the scene. In rapid succession the *U-95*, *U-147*, *U-70*, and *U-99* attacked. They claimed to have sunk many ships (actually two), and Berlin radio trumpeted the opening of the U-boat offensive. Combined with the air assault, said Dr. Goebbels's propagandist, the U-boat offensive was driving Britain to surrender.

Then on March 6, Doenitz heard from Prien again, a very brief transmission, but it reported on the discovery of Convoy OB293. Commander Kretschmer's *U-99* and Lieutenant Matz's *U-70* were sent to the area.

Kretschmer had the message on the night of March 6, and he made full speed to the area on the surface, arriving astern of the convoy early in the morning. He sighted Prien's *U-47* and tried to make radio contact, but as he did, a pair of British destroyers left the convoy and headed for the *U-99*. They had pinpointed his transmission with radio direction finders. Kretschmer took the *U-99* down fast; the destroyer *Wolverine* came up and dropped some depth charges, but soon lost asdic contact and did not regain it. Prien had also dived, and he also got away.

Lieutenant Matz had the message to join Prien at two

o'clock in the morning, and he moved, too, but his position and maneuvering brought him up in front of the convoy. The *U-70* was below the surface when the sound gear detected the noise of many ships' engines. The submarine surfaced and Matz attacked the sixty-five-hundred-ton tanker *Athelbeach*, and then the sixty-five-hundred-ton steamer *Delilian*. The crew abandoned the latter, although she did not sink.

Soon Lieutenant Matz saw an enormous vessel ahead. It was the twenty-thousand-ton whaling factory ship *Terje Viken*. She had been converted to become a tanker for wartime duty. The *U-70* fired three torpedoes at this big target, but all of them missed. Lieutenant Matz was just swinging the U-boat around to fire the stern tubes when Prien came up in the *U-47* and hit the *Terje Viken* with two torpedeos. She had many flotation compartments and so stayed afloat, but she was sorely hurt. Then Kretschmer arrived and put another torpedo into the whale ship and she capsized. Kretschmer then attacked another ship and was attacked in turn by an escort that forced him down. By the time he could surface, he had lost contact with the convoy. He saw Prien's *U-47*, and then they moved off in different directions to continue their hunting.

After the attack on the *Terje Viken*, the *U-70* then attacked the seventy-five-hundred-ton tanker *Mijdrecht*, which had stopped to pick up the crew of the *Delilian*. The *Mijdrecht* took the torpedo on the starboad side, but she was still moving. The captain saw the feather of the periscope of a submarine and put the helm over hard and rammed the *U-70*, damaging her so that she came out of balance and her stern stuck out of the water. The captain moved away far enough to shell the U-boat but did not make any hits with his deck gun.

But the *U-70* was badly damaged; her two periscopes were wrecked and the bridge was smashed. The conning tower was dented, the boat was taking water. Lieutenant Matz brought the boat to the surface, moved away from the convoy, and made repairs. Then he moved off. At 8:15 he was moving along at sixteen knots on the surface when the Flower-class corvette *Camellia* discovered the U-boat, forced the boat down, dropped depth charges, then lost asdic contact and moved off but brought up another corvette, the *Arbutus*, which made asdic contact at 9:25. The *Arbutus* made several depth charge runs; the U-boat went down to 260 feet, but the depth charges did some damage and water began coming into the boat.

Lieutenant Matz tried to escape, but the water kept coming in and the boat sank to 360 feet, and finally she sank until the depth went off the depth gauge (656 feet). The men began to hear ominous cracking sounds in the pressure hull, and no one knew how long it would be before the boat was crushed by the pressure.

So Matz realized that he had to surface since he could not maintain the trim under water, and he ordered the tanks blown. Just then the *Arbutus* came over the boat and dropped depth charges directly above her, set for 350 and 500 feet, but she was so far down that they did no damage. Finally she surfaced, the conning tower hatch was opened, and the six men at the top were sucked out of the boat by the changing pressure.

The *Arbutus* opened fire with its four-inch guns and then came up to ram. But when her captain saw that the men were not trying to fight but were jumping off the submarine, he dropped two Carley floats and stopped firing. He closed on the boat, which was still moving ahead under electric power. The crew came up, opening the vents. The boat went down then, so fast that two officers and eighteen men did not make it out of the boat on time. Skipper Matz and three other officers and twenty-two men survived, to become prisoners of war.

On March 7 Guenther Prien's *U-47* was heard reporting the course and speed and position of Convoy OB293, and then she was not heard from again. The reason was that the *U-47* was trapped below by the destroyer *Wolverine* and sunk with depth charges.

Kretschmer's *U-99* was lying low while Matz's boat was being sunk and Prien was being attacked but escaped, and when he cautiously brought the boat up, the sea was empty. He was ordered to meet a convoy spotted by Lieutenant Lemp in *U-110*, and so was Schepke in *U-100*. They found the convoy and on, March 16 Kretschmer attacked off the Faroes

Islands. He fired all his torpedoes and claimed to have sunk fifty-thousand tons of shipping, and then he disengaged and headed for his base at Saint-Nazaire.

Soon he found himself off the Lousy Banks, where floating mines had been seen earlier, so he intended to keep the area well to the starboard beam.

That night Kretschmer was getting some sleep. The bridge watch consisted of a watch officer, a pretty officer, and two seamen, and they were traveling on the surface. Suddenly the officer sighted a gun turret shimmering in the moonlight. A British destroyer was not more than a hundred yards away. It came out of the mist like an apparition.

Kretschmer had instructed his crew in such matters. "When reacting to objects sighted at night—stay surfaced" was his rule. But the young officer panicked and pressed the control button for an emergency dive. The bridge watch scrambled down the conning tower hatch, the hatch clanged, and the boat went down.

It was the fatal error.

The destroyer crew had not spotted the submarine on the surface. But once she got below, she was picked up by the destroyer's asdic apparatus, and the hunt was on.

Soon the depth charging began. The electric motors went out. Water broke through the pressure hull, and the crew lost control of the boat's equilibrium. She started toward the surface, came to the surface, and Kretschmer decided to keep her there. He saw one destroyer stopped within hailing distance, and a second on the opposite side. If he still had any torpedoes, he could have sunk both ships.

What were those destroyers doing?

They were picking up survivors of Schepke's *U-100*, which they had just destroyed. Suddenly the captains of the two destroyers realized that they had another U-boat within range, and both destroyers began to fire every gun they had. The U-boat heeled over under the rain of fire. Kretschmer ordered all men on deck, and they took cover in the lee of the conning tower. Soon the engineer officer reported that there was no chance of the U-boat submerging and escaping. Kretschmer ordered the men below again to get their personal belongings and to destroy valuable secret equipment.

Suddenly the U-boat began to sink. Inside the boat were the first lieutenant and the engineer officer. They blew all the valves to lighten the boat; the stern lifted, but the officers had to fight their way up the conning tower hatch, which was still submerged, and they were pulled onto the deck. The men on the stern had been swept off, had clung together, and been picked up by the *Vanoc*. The *Walker* closed and sent a boat. Kretschmer was afraid the British might capture the boat. The engineer officer went below to vent the after end of the boat so she would go down stern first. He did so, and the boat took him down, too, leaving Kretschmer and a band of survivors struggling in the water. The *Walker* came alongside and the British sailors helped the Germans up the nets. Two men were missing, perhaps dead from exhaustion or the icy cold of the sea. Kretschmer waited until the last to be saved.

That month of March 1941 six U-boats were sunk in the North Atlantic, and among them were three of the "stars" of the U-boat force, Prien, Kretschmer, and Schepke. Prien went down with his boat and was not seen again. Schepke was crushed against the periscope when the *Vanoc* rammed the *U-100*. Kretschmer survived, to go to prison camp, from which he conducted the only successful espionage agency the Germans had in England, and continued to send information when he was later transferred to Canada.

The British press was given the news, and pictures were printed of Kretschmer coming off the *Walker* at a British port. Doenitz wanted the news generally released in Germany, but Hitler and Goebbels would not agree; it was too dangerous to let the Germans think they were not winning the Battle of Britain. So the news was suppressed about the loss of the three "stars" for several weeks, and it was not until April that the Germans admitted Prien had been lost.

But in spite of the loss of these highly experienced captains, the battle went on, for Doenitz's wartime building program had now begun to bear fruit, and the five-hundred-ton Atlantic boats were beginning to come off the ways in significant numbers.

This spring there would be no break in the battle of Britain.

# CHAPTER 19

# *Blitz and Anti-Blitz*

In the beginning of 1941 Prime Minister Churchill felt the need to look into the future and see what might lie in store for Britain. The Germans were continuing the Battle of Britain and seemed unlikely to abandon the bombing. The situation at sea was grim and growing worse as more U-boats became available to Admiral Doenitz and the wolf pack technique was perfected. The expected invasion of England had not materialized in 1940, but that did not mean the attempt would not be made in the spring of 1941, and Churchill thought the Germans might try.

The prime minister began a study of current and expected air strengths of Britain and Germany in the spring. As he often did when faced with an abstruse subject, Churchill turned to Professor Frederick Lindemann, his scientific adviser, and his Statistical Branch. The Air Ministry and the Ministry of Economic Warfare were each also asked to prepare an estimate. When they came in, they were wildly different. Then Churchill turned the whole over to a distinguished jurist for adjudication, and at the end of January he had his report. It showed the Germans outnumbered the British in the air by four to three, but that British production was higher than Germany's.

The Germans at this point were concentrating on their coming invasion of Russia, and so much of the aircraft production was to be amassed for that effort, although the British did not know it. Meanwhile the air battle over Britain and the air and sea battle over the seas around Britain continued in what seemed to be undiminished force.

In the first two months, as has been seen, the air battle had slacked off due to the extremely bad weather. Cardiff, Swansea, and Portsmouth were badly bombed, and of course, the Blitz of London continued, but generally speaking, the civil defense service had a breathing spell. Then in March the Blitz began again in earnest with the new series of attacks on the port cities of Plymouth, Merseyside, and the Clyde River.

The month of April brought the heavy raids. The British were still congratulating themselves on the sinking of six U-boats in March when April brought an entirely new air assault. On April 8 Coventry was hit hard again. Once more, it was as if the clock were turned back: officialdom was hardly more ready for the attack than it had been the first time.

Portsmouth was blitzed again with hundreds of tons of bombs, and once again, the social services were lacking. One positive change had been made; the old-fashioned system of locally autonomous fire services was changed and the National Fire Service emerged, which could concentrate men and equipment where they were needed without unraveling red tape.

Finally, the government of London and other cities decided that the Blitz would be around for a while and a national shelter policy was inaugurated, which resulted in considerable improvement of bomb shelters.

Bristol was attacked again on April 12. London was heavily attacked on April 16 and April 17 with indiscriminate flinging of bombs on the city, and twenty-three hundred people were killed and more than three thousand seriously wounded.

If the British had thought the Blitz was winding down, then the attacks of April had to convince them that it was not. Plymouth, for example, was attacked for more than a week, from April 21 to April 29, and the damage to the city was extreme.

The Civil Defense Corps had learned some lessons from earlier bombings. One was to set up a smoke screen, which hid an area from the bombers. The trouble with the smoke screens is that they smoke up the whole community, and the acrid smell persisted for days. But they had their value in protecting industry.

So did decoy fires, called "starfish" by the Civil Defense Corps. These were fires set in the general area of an important manufacturing plant, but well away from the production facilities, so that the Luftwaffe would think the fire area was the real thing and bomb it. The trouble with the decoy fires was that they brought the enemy over the populated city, and the inhabitants suffered.

The last of that spring's accelerated raids on Merseyside were concentrated on the Liverpool docks beginning May 1. The area was bombed heavily for seven consecutive nights; more than seventy-five thousand people were made homeless and three thousand people were killed or wounded. Almost half the 144 shipping berths in the Mersey were made unusable at least temporarily, and for some time shipping was sorely hurt, with the tonnage landed cut to about a quarter of the usual. Had the Luftwaffe persisted at Liverpool, they might have knocked that port out altogether, which could have been a disaster for England, but they moved on to Hull, where they bombed out forty thousand people, wrecked the engineering works, which was out of action for two months, and destroyed great quantities of stored food. Belfast was hit again, too, but the saving grace for England was that the Germans did not know what they had accomplished, or where, and their bombing was not only indiscriminate, but blind and with no persistent plan.

At sea this spring when the British convoys began to make wide detours to the north, the U-boats followed them as far as the sixtieth parallel and continued to sink ships. So the British moved the convoy routes again, this time southwest of Rockall, and soon the U-boats were also moving south. They formed patrol lines between Iceland and Rockall, and off Saint Kilda. One night in the middle of April the U-boats found Convoy SC26, and sank fourteen ships.

The British still suffered from a shortage of escort vessels, but the corvettes were beginning to come off the ways, corvettes and frigates, small ships designed specifically for escort work, light, fast, and maneuverable vessels equipped with better underwater detection gear and depth charge throwers.

Admiral Doenitz was getting some 750-ton boats now, and these larger ones were sent farther afield, to Africa, where the concentration of shipping was heavy and British defenses were weak. Early in March the *U-106* and *U-105* were trailing a convoy they had picked up at Freetown, Sierra Leone. SL68 consisted of fifty-eight ships, guarded by four destroyers, an auxiliary cruiser, and the battleship *Malaya*. The convoy steered west, toward the Cape Verde Islands, and for eight days until March 17, the two U-boats trailed the convoy; then on the night of the seventeenth, *U-106* moved in to attack at periscope depth. The captain fired all his bow tubes. The *U-105* also attacked. In two nights the submarines sank seven ships, and on the nineteenth the convoy was dispersed. Only when the *U-106* returned to Lorient in June did the captain learn that one of his torpedoes had hit the battleship *Malaya*, which had gone across the Atlantic for repair at the Brooklyn Navy Yard in New York.

So the Battle of Britain and supply went on that spring. Between March and May the U-boats sank 142 ships, totalling 818,000 tons of shipping, and the Luftwaffe and surface raiders doubled that figure. These were difficult days for the British. Early in May Admiral Doenitz moved his wolf packs west, and one found Convoy HX126, which yielded nine ships.

In the air battle, the Germans kept using their various beams, and the British became more adept at deflecting them. On the night of May 8 the Luftwaffe planned two attacks by KGr100, using X beams, one on the Rolls-Royce factory at Derby and one on Nottingham. The beams were set on Derby, but the British bent them, which distorted the whole attack. Some of the bombs hit Nottingham, but only because the Germans were guided by some small fires set the night before, and they missed Derby altogether, putting their bombs into the countryside. The Germans confidently claimed that they had destroyed the Rolls-Royce factory, but anyone who worked there knew differently—the Germans did not even come near the place. Two hundred and thirty high-explosive bombs and many incendiaries fell on the farmland, killing two chickens.

On May 10 Prime Minister Churchill was visiting friends in the country. It was the weekend, and his host had arranged for a showing of a new Marx Brothers comedy film. During the film Churchill learned of the bombing of London that night, which was unusually severe. It was primarily an incendiary raid, which started two thousand fires. The bombers dropped enough high explosives also to smash 150 water mains, which seriously plagued the fire fighters. The fires burned and burned all night long, and at six o'clock the next morning they were still burning. Four were still burning on the night of May 13. It was, as it turned out to be, the most destructive raid to London of the entire Battle of Britain, knocking out five docks and seventy-one key points of transportation and communications and important factories. All but one of the main railroad stations in the city were blocked for several weeks, and the rail routes were not all opened until early June. More than three thousand people were killed or wounded, and the raid also destroyed the House of Commons.

At sea, the British began to get more help from the Americans. In May 1940, after Denmark was occupied by the Germans, the American government was asked by the local government of the Danish possession of Greenland to protect the colony from German occupation. The Germans had already established a weather-reporting station on the east coast, which was very important to the Luftwaffe operations over England. So that year the Americans established "an unofficial protectorate" over Greenland.

But by March 1941 the Americans had the disquieting news that the Germans were planning to build an airfield and base and air squadron on Greenland. If this happened, then the Germans would indeed control the North Atlantic, and the British lifeline would be threatened. So the Americans sent an expedition to Greenland and signed an agreement with the Danish government in exile taking on a protectorate, a matter made known to the Germans.

The United States had also in July 1940 declared its intention to defend the Western Hemisphere against foreign incursion. On April 18, 1941, Admiral Ernest J. King, commander of the Atlantic Fleet, marked out "the western hemisphere" for defense purposes. It ran from Iceland west to the international date line and included Greenland, the Azores, the Gulf of Saint Lawrence, the Bahama islands, the Caribbean Sea, and the Gulf of Mexico.

And here was the shocker for the Germans:

"Entrance into the Western Hemisphere by naval ships or aircraft of belligerent powers other than those powers having sovereignty over territory in the Western Hemisphere is to be viewed as possibly actuated by an unfriendly interest toward shipping or territory in the Western Hemisphere."

So British ships could sail in these waters and British planes patrol, but German U-boats and German aircraft could not, lest they bring down action by the Americans.

At the same time the U.S. Atlantic Fleet was reorganized to create task forces for patrol of various areas, and to stop the Germans from building any bases in Greenland. This was the special mission of the Greenland Patrol.

Thus frustrated, Doenitz thought he saw opportunity off Greenland and off Newfoundland, and decided to risk the American wrath by sending boats there. Early in May five U-boats that were already stationed off the south of Iceland moved farther west and found a convoy, from which they sank nine ships and damaged three. Two other boats then were sent to reinforce them off South Greenland, and the whole group moved to the southwest, found another convoy, and sank nine more ships.

Admirals Raeder and Doenitz were disturbed by the extension of American activity in behalf of the British and asked Hitler to give greater range to the U-boats and let them operate off the American coast as well as in mid-Atlantic waters. They also asked that American ships be declared fair game if they were operating without lights. But Hitler did not want to run the danger of bringing the Americans into the war just as he was about to start operations against Russia, so he refused them any new latitude.

By June, Doenitz had thirty-five boats at sea, and more coming along. In the three months of March, April, and May, the Luftwaffe sank 179 ships or 545,000 tons.

To increase the pressure on the British, the Germans sent the forty-thousand-ton battleship *Bismarck* into the Atlantic with the cruiser *Prinz Eugen*. The news of this sailing electrified the naval world, particularly America, for the most modern American battleship in commission then was the *West Virginia*, with fourteen-inch guns, and she was twenty years old.

Then came an incident of which the British made light, but one that indicated the state of mind of Hitler in that spring of 1941. Hitler had already declared the British to be beaten, and he had spent ten months trying to force them to accept his European suzerainty, without visible result. Hitler now had other matters on his mind, especially his "holy crusade" against Communist Russia, which he was ready to pursue. The necessity of maintaining so much force against the British was a great nuisance, underlined by what was happening in the Mediterranean. Yugoslavia had refused to join the Tripartite Pact and had been crushed. Greece was next on the agenda; all this was preliminary to the invasion of Russia, which should bring about control of the oil of the Caucasus, entry to the Middle East, and an unlimited supply of slave labor for the Third Reich.

All this could be easy, Hitler reasoned, were it not for the continued resistance of the pesky British.

This reasoning was often aired at the Hitler luncheon table, to which came officials from the army, navy, and Luftwaffe, plus party favorites and administrators, whoever happened that day to be in the chancellery or wherever Hitler was lunching. One frequenter of the table was Rudolf Hess, who was deputy führer, reich minister without portfolio, and who had several other titles. Hess was notable as one of the original Nazis. It was he who had accompanied Hitler to prison after the aborted Munich Beer Hall putsch, and it was Hess to whom Hitler had dictated *Mein Kampf*, the book that in the 1920s showed the wave of the German future.

In recent years, Hess had been eclipsed by events. Primarily he was a Nazi party functionary, and for Hitler the party had been displaced by the *Oberkommando* Wehrmacht, the three great elements of the German fighting machine.

Hess still commanded Hitler's intimacy, but he had very little to do, and much time to think.

So Rudolf Hess developed the idea that he, alone, could do what Hermann Goering and the Luftwaffe and Admiral Doenitz and the U-boat corps could not do—persuade the British to make peace.

Hess knew that Prime Minister Churchill was the implacable enemy of Hitler and the Third Reich. But he also knew from neutral reports, because Britain was still a free country and opinions were still voiced, that there was dissatisfaction in Britain with Churchill's rule (a fact much exaggerated in Germany), and he knew that at one point the former King Edward VIII had shown great partiality for Hitler's Germany.

So why would not the ruling family have similar feelings? The way to get to the British people, around the difficult Churchill, was to approach King George VI. Hess believed he had a way to do this. Earlier he had met the Duke of Hamilton in connection with the Olympic Games, and they had become more than nodding acquaintances. He knew that the duke was an intimate of the king's. This suggested the avenue of approach. He would fly to Scotland, where the duke's lands were located. The duke would give him access to the king. The king would prove reasonable, and presto, peace would come between Germany and Britain, and Britain, instead of being an enemy, would be an ally.

So on May 10, 1941, Rudolf Hess had flown his own plane to Scotland, and parachuted near the Duke of Hamilton's estate. He had been slightly injured in landing and taken to a military hospital by people who thought he was a German Luftwaffe pilot. There he had demanded to see the Duke of Hamilton, and had identified himself. The duke came, and Rudolf Hess had his first shock. The duke offered no sympathy to the project, and instead went off to telephone the prime minister with the news. Hess was placed under guard, and the duke telephoned Prime Minister Churchill, who was an old friend.

Churchill stoutly refused to have anything to do with the matter. Hess was a prisoner of war. He was moved about, questioned, and ultimately confined to the Tower of London, where he spent the rest of the war.

The Hess mission was a great embarrassment to Hitler. It took a few days for Propaganda Minister Goebbels to get over the shock. Then he issued a statement to the press:

"It seemed that Party Member Hess lived in a state of hallucination, as a result of which he felt he would bring about an understanding between England and Germany. The National Socialist Party regrets that this idealist fell victim to his hallucination. This, however, will have no effect on the continuance of the war which has been forced on Germany."

So the war went on, apparently with undiminished vigor. The *Bismarck* and the *Prinz Eugen* were out, and the battleships *Scharnhorst* and *Gneisenau* were in Brest. It looked as though the Germans were preparing to scour the Atlantic, a development very dark indeed for the British Royal Navy.

On the morning of May 24, Admiral Sir John Tovey's Home Fleet battle cruiser *Hood* and the battleship *Prince of Wales* made contact with the *Bismarck*. In the battle that followed, the *Bismarck* sank the *Hood* with a single salvo of its giant guns, at least one shell penetrating the ship's magazine and causing her to blow up. But the *Bismarck* had also been hit, and thereafter, although she escaped, she trailed oil, leaving a telltale track. She was found by a British squadron and by planes from the carrier *Ark Royal*. The planes torpedoed the ship and slowed her down, and the British battleships *Rodney* and *King George V* sank her on May 27.

The movement of the German submarines to the western side of the Atlantic that spring created a new crisis for the British, because the British escorts from the United Kingdom could only cover the convoys for a quarter of the distance to Halifax, Nova Scotia. With those convoy sinkings in May, the British realized they somehow had to extend their protection or the lifeline would be cut. What was needed as soon as possible was escort from one side of the Atlantic to the other.

In May the Canadian government agreed to undertake the western escort, and so there came into being the continuous escort over the entire length of the Atlantic voyage, although it was still not adequate to stop U-boat incursions.

The first step in the intervention of the United States had

been the declaration of the western hemisphere zone, which was denied to the Germans. Now the supply of American munitions and aircraft increased dramatically.

President Roosevelt announced that he had allocated funds to build fifty-eight shipyards and 200 more ships for the Atlantic route. The sinews of war were indeed being strengthened.

Since January, the British and American high commands had carried on a series of discussions for joint defense of the Atlantic Ocean, and framing a world strategy, which envisaged the war spreading also to the Pacific, with Japan as the principal antagonist. It was agreed then in principle that if this state of affairs came to pass, the war against Germany would take first place, and the war against Japan would have to await the defeat of Hitler.

The British, Canadians, and Americans began preparing bases on British Empire soil for American naval escorts and air forces. One of these important bases was at Argentia in Newfoundland, and bases were also selected in the United Kingdom. The Americans were building to entry in the war. The British were building up their military and naval forces in Iceland, which they had occupied when Denmark was invaded by the Germans. Iceland became a separate naval command, extending the range of the surface escorts to thirty-five degrees west longitude. Still there was a gap to the west, which was not covered by the British or the Canadians or the American surface ships, and the long-range bombers that would ultimately help here were not yet in evidence in the spring of 1941.

Another area that caused great concern in London was the Azores Islands. This Portuguese colony was within the American western hemispheric zone, but there were indications in the spring of 1941 that the Germans were planning to seize the Azores and build a U-boat and air base there. Since these islands lie near the center of the Atlantic Ocean, if the Germans could achieve that end, it would give them an enormous advantage. The Portuguese government, while ostensibly neutral, was worried about the German plans and told the British. Churchill ordered plans for an expedition to occupy the Azores and the Portuguese Cape Verde Islands as well as the Spanish Canary Islands if Hitler moved into Spain. All these moves by Hitler had been telegraphed, and seemed to be possible dangers in that winter of 1941.

On May 22, however, came a major change in the war. That was the day that Field Marshal Kesselring shifted the headquarters of his air fleet to Posen, Poland. Within the month the entire Luftwaffe force that had been fighting against Britain was removed from the French and low country and Norwegian airfields and sent to the east for participation in Operation Barbarossa, the attack on Russia. The Battle of Britain was over, and the war was entering a new phase. The battle in the air had cost the British civilian casualties of forty-three thousand killed and fifty thousand seriously wounded, or a total of nearly one hundred thousand civilians. The shipping losses were enormous and would continue that way, but this was the only manifestation of the war in Britain proper. Hitler had turned south to the Mediterranean, and east to Russia.

Hitler believed it was but a temporary respite. The Luftwaffe had been ordered to be ready to shift back to the Western European bases in six weeks time after the beginning of Operation Barbarossa. Hitler and his generals estimated that it would take no longer than six weeks to defeat Russia, and then the Luftwaffe and the U-boat arm could finish the Battle of Britain victoriously.

In the event, however, affairs did not work out that way, and nearly three years were to pass before Britain again felt the onslaught of German might from the air. In effect, the Battle of Britain was over and the British had won.

# NOTES

## 1 Reality and Myth—the Truth About Air Power

Much of the information for the first chapter of the book comes from studies I made for *Goering's War* at the Imperial War Museum and the German military archives in Freiburg, West Germany.

## 2 The Respite of Phony War—and Its End

*The Battle of Britain* was central to this chapter, as were the Goering biographical studies. Winston Churchill's *Their Finest Hour* was also important, and Shirer's *The Rise and Fall of the Third Reich*.

## 3 The German Juggernaut

*The Rise and Fall of the Third Reich* was useful here, as well as Churchill's *Their Finest Hour* and R. J. Overy's *Air War*. Harold Faber's *The Luftwaffe, a History* was also helpful.

## 4 The Battle of the Convoys

*The Battle of Britain* was useful here, particularly the day-by-day listing of attacks and air battles in the appendixes. Also, Peter Townsend's personal account of the Battle of Britain, *Duel of Eagles*, was helpful to set the scene.

### 5 The Secret Radio Beam

R. V. Jones's own story of the Wizard War was essential to this chapter, plus Churchill's account of the progress of the battle.

### 6 The Air Struggle Begins

*Their Finest Hour* was the source for the opening of the chapter. The Mosley biography of Goering was the source for the quotation about the paucity of aircraft in the Luftwaffe. *The Battle of Britain* was useful for the chronology and story of the fighting in the air.

### 7 Crucial Day

*The Battle of Britain* was important to this chapter. So was Peter Townsend's account.

### 8 After Black Thursday, What?

Sommerfeldt was important in the picture of Goering in this chapter. The story of the battle is from *The Battle of Britain*, Peter Townsend, and the Churchill book, *Their Finest Hour*.

### 9 "The Decisive Phase . . ."–Goering

The Goering quotation is from Lange's *Der Reichsmarschal im Kriege*. The material about Dowding's activity is from *The Battle of Britain*, and Churchill's comes from his own books. Some of the tales come from Townsend.

### 10 The Bombing of London

The count of invasion barges is from *The Battle of Britain*. The account of Goering's activities is from Lange. Shirer's observations are detailed in *The Rise and Fall of the Third Reich*. Churchill's activities are detailed in *Their Finest Hour*. Correspondent Murrow's observations come from his book.

### 11 London Can Take It

The Goering story is from Lange and from *The Battle of Britain*. The story of the king's escapade is from *The Battle of Britain*. Goebbels's observations are from *The Goebbels Diaries 1939-41*. The stories about the burned-out shops are from Murrow.

The running story of the delay in the decision about Operation Sea Lion comes from Field Marshal Keitel's *Memoirs*, published by Stein and Day in America. Goering's reactions are from Lange and other biographies. The stories of the Nippy trainees are from Tom Harrisson's *Living Through the Blitz*.

## 12   The Great Air Battle

The story of Churchill's visit to Group 11's control center is from *Their Finest Hour*. The story of operations is from Townsend and the *Battle of Britain*.

## 13   The War Winds Down

The tale of Anthony Eden is from *Their Finest Hour*. The Erpro stories are from *The Battle of Britain* and *Die Luftwaffe*. Murrow's tales are from his book.

## 14   The Scene Shifts

The story of the Italians is from *The Battle of Britain* and from records of the Royal Navy in the Public Records Office. The story of the Knickebein beam is from Dr. Jones's book and from Churchill's *Their Finest Hour*. The story of the bombing of Coventry is from the Harrisson book. The story of the *Scheer* is from the records at the Public Records Office.

## 15   The New Sea War

The material about the sea aspect of the Battle of Britain is from Churchill's *Their Finest Hour*, Morison, and Busch. The story of the sinking of *U-32* is from the Admiralty files in the Public Records Office. The quotations from Churchill come from *Their Finest Hour*.

## 16   Southampton

The material about the Blitz is from Harrisson. The story of the bombing of Southampton is from that source as well.

### 17 Defeat Into Victory

The Murrow book was the source of the tales about the reporters. The Harrisson book gave the details of the bombing of Portsmouth and Southampton. The table showing shipping losses is from the Churchill book, *Their Finest Hour*. The story of Churchill's visit to Plymouth was told in *The Battle of Britain*.

### 18 The Battle Continued

The story of the Merseyside raids is from Harrisson. The material about the U-boats is from the Admiralty files in the Public Records Office. The Goering story comes from Busch and Morison and Fraenkel. The story of the end of the three star captains is from the Admiralty files in the Public Records Office.

### 19 Blitz and Anti-Blitz

The story of Churchill's activity here is from *The Grand Alliance*, volume III in the Churchill story of World War II. Busch supplied the U-boat materials. The stories of the beams come from the Jones book. The story of Hess comes from Churchill. The material about the American efforts comes from Morison and Churchill. The story of the *Bismarck* is from the Admiralty files of the Public Records Office.

# BIBLIOGRAPHY

Busch, Harald. *U-Boats at War*. New York: Ballantine, 1955.

Butler, Ewan. *Marshal Without Glory*. London: Tandem, 1973.

Churchill, Winston. *The Grand Alliance*. Boston: Houghton Mifflin, 1950.

———. *Their Finest Hour*. Boston: Houghton Mifflin, 1949.

Faber, Harald, ed. *Luftwaffe, a History*. New York: Times Books, 1977.

Fraenkel, Heinrich, and Roger Manvel. *Hermann Goering*. Herrsching: Manfred Pawlak. Verlagsellschaft, MBH, West Germany. 1962.

Frank, Wolfgang. *Sea Wolves*. New York: Ballantine, 1955.

Frischauer, Willi. *Goering*. London: Odham's Press, undated.

Gutzbach, Erich. *Hermann Goering*. London: Hurst and Blackett, 1939.

Harrisson, Tom. *Living Through the Blitz*. New York: Schocken Books, 1976.

Hough, Richard, and Dennis Richards. *The Battle of Britain*. New York: Norton, 1989.

Hoyt, Edwin P. *Goering's War*. London: Robert Hale, 1988.

Jones, R. V. *The Wizard War*. New York: Coward McCann and Geoghegan, 1978.

Lange, Eitel. *Der Reichsmarschal im Kriege*. Stuttgart, West Germany: C. E. Schwab Verlag, 1950.

Lee, Asher. *Goering the Leader*. New York: Ballantine, 1972.

Manvell, Roger. *Hermann Goering*. London: New English Library, 1968.

Mason, Herbert Molloy. *The Rise of the Luftwaffe*. New York: Dial Press, 1973.

Morison, Samuel E. *The Battle of the Atlantic*. Boston: Atlantic Little Brown, 1975.

Mosley, Leonard. *The Reich Marshal*. New York: Doubleday, 1974.

Murray, Williamson. *Luftwaffe*. London: Geoerge Allen and Unwin, 1985.

Murrow, Edward R. *This Is London*. New York: Schocken Books, 1941.

Overy, A. J. *The Air War*. New York: Stein and Day, 1980.

Shirer, William L. *The Rise and Fall of the Third Reich*. New York: Simon and Schuster, 1960.

Sommerfeldt, Martin H. *Hermann Goering, Ein Lebensbild*. Berlin: Mittler & Sohn, 1934.

Townsend, Peter. *Duel of Eagles*. New York: Simon and Schuster, 1969.

# INDEX